1992

THE FACTS ABOUT
ADOLESCENT DRUG ABUSE

TITLES IN THE FACTS ABOUT ... SERIES

THE FACTS ABOUT ADOLESCENT DRUG ABUSE

JOHN DAVIES AND NIALL COGGANS

CASSELL

Cassell Educational Limited
Villiers House
41/47 Strand
London WC2N 5JE

First published 1991

British Library Cataloguing in Publication Data

Davies, John
    The facts about adolescent drug abuse. – (The Facts About ... series)
    1. Great Britain. Adolescents. Drug abuse
    I. Title II. Coggans, Niall
    362.2930835

ISBN 0–304–32274–1 (hardback)
        0–304–32280–6 (paperback)

Typeset by Fakenham Photosetting Limited, Fakenham, Norfolk
Printed and bound in Great Britain by Biddles Ltd, Guildford and King's Lynn

CONTENTS

Contents

SERIES FOREWORD

The idea for this series came from an awareness that much of the media hype, and some of the professional practice, relating to major social problems involving children and adolescents was singularly ill-informed. At the same time there was a notable lack of short, accessible summaries of the relevant research data by which people could inform themselves.

Not surprisingly, the conclusions that are drawn from a careful consideration of the evidence challenge many generally held assumptions – at all levels of popular and professional concern.

Bill Gillham

ACKNOWLEDGEMENT

Thanks are gratefully given to Judith Gillham for editorial assistance in the detailed preparation of the manuscript.

INTRODUCTION

The purpose of this book is to encourage new perspectives on the problems created by the use of illicit mind-altering substances and the phenomenon known as 'addiction'. It is aimed at drug workers, teachers, social workers, health professionals, parents of teenage children and concerned adults in all walks of life.

Whilst particular prominence is given to the use and misuse of drugs by young people, the issues surrounding teenagers' use of illicit drugs go beyond this specific age-group. Teenagers are not uniquely afflicted by drug problems; by and large regular heavy use of illicit drugs by youngsters of school age is rare, though there is considerable variability between different geographical areas. Consequently, the book argues for new conceptions of addiction overall and new approaches to coping with the problems sometimes caused by drugs *in general*, even though the specific problems of teenage misuse may be of particular concern to us.

Central to the theme of the book are certain stereotyped and inaccurate beliefs in general circulation concerning the nature of addiction and the helplessness of 'addicts' in the face of pharmacological forces which take over their lives. This mechanistic view of addiction is false but is sustained by press and media coverage, which regularly describes drug use in these terms. However, research evidence shows that the notion of the 'helpless addict' is functional, and that it serves clear purposes for people who are confronted by drug problems in some form. In other words, it is a useful type of explanation rather than a literal truth.

In contrast to the stereotype, an alternative view is presented here which sees drug use deriving from dynamic and purposeful, if unwise, choices made by individuals faced with particular alternatives. Consequently, understanding drug use requires a primary focus on the *motives and intentions of people*, rather than on the pharmacological properties of substances. Unfortunately, many policy decisions concerned with drugs and drug use are basically drug focused, the current 'war on drugs' in the USA being a prime example. It is argued here that such a war will never succeed in stamping out drugs, any more than Prohibition succeeded in removing alcohol. Instead, the economic gains from drug trafficking are increased by such a policy option, encouraging ever-greater risks by those concerned, and actually stimulating crime and shootings on the street. The side-effects of such a policy can thus be more damaging than the drugs themselves.

On the assumption that drugs cannot in fact be eradicated, a harm-reduction philosophy is urged, which requires the re-thinking of certain beliefs about the nature of drug misuse and addiction, and replacement of stereotyped beliefs about helpless junkies and substances that instantly corrupt by something based on firmer evidence.

Only by opting for a policy which copes positively with drug problems can drug misuse be monitored and controlled for the benefit of individuals and of society as a whole, rather than driven underground, at which level little effective intervention is possible. The alternative strategy, based on more and harsher penalties, encourages the type of crime-related drug use that we most wish to avoid, whilst making it less likely that those experiencing problems from their drug misuse will come forward to receive the health care they need.

1
WHAT IS A DRUG PROBLEM?

During the last decade, problems associated with the use of illegal drugs for pleasure (or what has come to be known as the 'recreational' use of drugs) have achieved a degree of prominence which is unprecedented. Fears about the involvement of teenagers and even 10- and 11-year-olds with substances associated with dependence and addiction have grown out of all proportion, compared with other perennial problems, and there is concern at all levels, from parents to governments, about the dangers of what is perceived as a new menace. The fear that a whole generation might be wiped out, and that the very fabric of society as we know it might be destroyed by chemical dependence, has been voiced on both sides of the Atlantic (Woodiwiss, 1988; Trebach, 1987). Growing fear and concern have been mirrored by increased coverage in the press and in television programmes, and by national anti-drug campaigns carrying messages of death and disaster.

In terms of hard evidence, there is no doubt that drugs are now more readily available than ever before, and in greater variety. The range of substances used by young people has expanded radically from the 'traditional' drugs of protest such as cannabis and LSD (lysergic acid diethylamide), and now includes all the feared substances previously held to have attraction only for ageing jazz musicians and other marginal groups.

This increased involvement with illicit mood- and consciousness-changing drugs is reflected in official statistics. For example, the current number of Home Office-registered addicts to heroin and cocaine stands at something in the region of 14,800 compared to 437 in 1960. In that year there were 94 notified cases of heroin addiction compared with over 12,000 in 1989. Cannabis offences have risen from 235 to 33,669 over the same period (all figures from Royal College of Psychiatrists report: *Drug Scenes*, 1987; Home Office Statistical Bull-

3

etin, 1990). At the same time, there has been a real increase in the numbers attending clinics and hospitals with drug-related health problems, as well as a massive rise in the number of seizures of illicit drugs (and in the quantities seized) by customs officials, and a perceived shift in public opinion towards seeing drug abuse as a major cause of theft and crime on the streets.

At an individual level, tragedy as a consequence of drug use features regularly in the popular press. There is no question that numbers of people die each year, some of them in their late teens or early twenties, in a manner that implicates drug use. In addition, the American experience with cocaine over the last three years is regularly brought to our attention, with street shootings and killings becoming an everyday occurrence in centres such as Washington. The warning is regularly issued by American drug-enforcement officers that a similar experience lies in store for us unless we react quickly, and learn the best ways to stamp out this menace from the USA experience. Finally, the new super-drug 'crack' is already in our midst, having properties so volatile and compelling that, according to some experts, all or most of those who try it are instantly addicted (Browne, 1988; McGinty and Hamilton, 1990), a claim which if true would be most alarming. Even as these words are written, the amphetamine-based drug 'ice' is appearing, with properties that are said to be more addictive still.

Faced with facts like these, it is small wonder that a kind of frozen hysteria takes hold of the minds of many parents and teachers at the very mention of the word 'drugs'. Illicit-drug use is definitely a problem, and all the signs indicate that more people are going to become involved as time passes, unless there is a radical shift in direction. The question naturally arises, however, as to whether the current drug experience is totally new, without precedent, or whether it represents a recent expansion of a problem which has been lurking in the background for some considerable time.

THE HISTORY OF DRUG USE: NEW DRUGS FOR OLD

In fact, there are a number of contemporary accounts of the use of drugs for purposes that would now be considered illegal, which document their widespread use throughout recorded history. Such accounts refer to the availability of opium over the shop-counter in the Fenland districts of the UK, the widespread use of opiate-based cough medicines for children, the non-prescribed use of laudanum as a pick-me-up or to steady the nerves, and many more examples spanning the last 150 years (*Drug Scenes*, 1987). In addition, many notable figures are known to have made use of, and in some cases been dependent upon, mind-altering substances, including well-known poets and artists as well as more conventional and less bohemian individuals, politicians and public figures not normally associated with illegal activities. Even Conan Doyle's fictitious genius, Sherlock Holmes, had his cachet increased rather than diminished by cocaine addiction.

The above remarks refer, of course, to drugs other than alcohol, the use and abuse of which has a history going back as far as one wishes to investigate, embracing virtually all cultures. For the present, it is sufficient to say that at various times in our history, many drugs which are currently illegal unless prescribed, including Class A drugs (i.e. opiates), have been available on general demand, sometimes offered for purchase by all and sundry across shop-counters, or from the corner grocer's rather than the pharmacist or doctor. Along with alcoholic beverages, we have employed these to quieten our children when they coughed too much or were unable to sleep; to calm ourselves in times of stress or anxiety; to lift our spirits in times of depression; as an aid to weight loss; and to help with asthmatic breathing difficulties. The amphetamine-based drugs which caused such a furore when used by mods and rockers in the 1960s, and whose use is once again troubling us in the form of the acid-house and ecstasy craze, were given to soldiers in combat during World War II to keep them functioning under conditions of fatigue and stress. They have also been used by mountaineers, racing cyclists and other sportsmen and women. Lorry drivers use them so that they can tackle long journeys without sleep (hence their colloquial name 'coast-to-coast'), and they are employed by students as an aid in all-night swotting sessions. They have even been fed to chickens to improve their rate of laying (*Drug Scenes*, 1987). The use of mind-altering substances is not new. So what is all the fuss about?

On the one hand we may take comfort from the fact that the problem is neither new nor strange, and that there is a past from which lessons can be learned. On the other hand, there are clear differences between the 'then' and the 'now' scenarios which have to be taken into account. Firstly, experimentation and occasional use of illicit drugs is now fairly common. Recent studies suggest that one in five children may have tried an illicit drug at some time, though this bald statistic is by no means as alarming as it appears, as we shall see in a later chapter. However, this is only one manifestation of the fact that illicit drugs are now more readily available than at any other time in our history. Consequently, more people have some drug experience; and at the tip of the iceberg there are more people with a visible drug problem. In addition, many of these are substantially younger than the stereotypical drug addict of the fifties.

Furthermore, there is a proliferation in the range of substances currently available for illicit use. This includes a vast range of minor tranquillizers, painkillers and other pharmaceuticals which can be adulterated, or dissolved, or otherwise prepared for use in unintended ways, some of which form a regular component of the heroin user's poly-drug diet in parts of the country where the heroin supply is limited or variable. In addition, new synthetics and new forms of old drugs are forever arriving on the scene. These include the notorious cocaine-derivative 'crack', and various amphetamine-based drugs including 'ecstasy', a form of methamphetamine. The amphetamine molecule is particularly adaptable and offers almost endless scope for development. The prospect of new and untried designer drugs is particularly worrying, since the search for new (and consequently not classified) drugs has produced a number of substances with lethal side-effects in the USA. Finally, we are faced with the prospect of exotics like PCP (phencyclidine), amyl nitrate, and others, whose pedigree is so short that they offer an unknown and terrifying prospect. Add to this the implication of AIDS with intravenous drug use, and there is no longer any doubt as to why the current upward trend in illicit drug use is a cause of major concern.

WHAT ARE DRUGS?

So far we have acknowledged the fact that the illicit use of drugs is a genuine cause for concern, and that anyone who looks into the issue need not search far before encountering some harrowing individual cases. However, we have also noted that drug use without medical advice is nothing new, that at different times and in different places drugs which we currently view with fear and alarm have been widely used, and indeed socially sanctioned. At the same time, our own alcohol and tobacco are viewed with extreme disapproval in other parts of the world. It should be apparent, therefore, that an integral part of the drug problem is the way in which different substances are perceived, and there is no absolute geographical or historical consensus on this matter. The question is whether a classification of drugs exists which can encompass these differences in cultural perspective and, if so, what its nature might be.

Many books give various classifications of substances, and no purpose is served here by providing yet another detailed attempt at the task. One of the more comprehensible accounts is given in *Drug Scenes* (1987). It is sufficient to note here that no simple pharmacological or physiological fact can provide the basis for a classification which distinguishes the drugs regarded in the West as illegal from those such as alcohol and tobacco that we accept and enjoy, or at least tolerate without legal sanctions. Consequently, any classification that distinguishes illicit drugs from approved or accepted 'recreational' drugs must be in terms of the ways in which we think about drugs, and our emotional reactions when the word 'drug' is used. For example, whilst the pharmacology of various drugs is fairly well understood, and in some instances extremely well understood, there is no simple pharmacological dimension equivalent to 'dangerousness' which separates the legal drugs such as tobacco and alcohol from the 'serious' drugs like cocaine and heroin. Although we habitually view drinking and smoking calmly, albeit perhaps with some dismay from time to time, our view of heroin and cocaine tends towards hysteria, based on a belief that in some simple and identifiable way these drugs are clearly more dangerous. In fact, no scientific evidence exists to support this general distinction. A moment's reflection is sufficient to convince even the most sceptical that tobacco and alcohol can hardly be recommended on the basis that they are harmless. In fact, whilst estimates of deaths due to tobacco suggest a figure of around 100,000 per annum, and perhaps one-third of that number due to alcohol, recorded deaths due to the direct effects of illicit drug use currently number about 400 per annum.

In addition, there are some remarkable paradoxes inherent in our habitual ways of thinking about drugs. For example, if one discounts deaths due to accidental overdoses, the medical evidence tends to support the proposition that prolonged regular use of heroin has very few deleterious health consequences, provided that the dangers arising from impure or dangerous adulterants and from dangerous injecting practices are removed. By contrast, prolonged regular use of either alcohol or tobacco has the most serious health effects in the long term deriving from the drugs themselves.

In a psychological sense, therefore, and regardless of pharmacological categorizations, the word 'drug' refers less to a functionally distinct set of mind-altering substances than to an arbitrary grouping of substances which are seen as 'bad'. The reasons why they are seen as bad, whilst other psychotropic substances are tolerated or even approved, are cultural and historical, rather than scientific. And it is worth repeating that there is no cross-cultural or historical unanimity about which substances are approved and which are illegal. Alcohol is an illicit drug in some parts of the world, whilst the use of opium or cannabis is approved or tolerated.

In Western societies, however, a legal distinction underpins the separation between alcohol and tobacco and the illicit drugs, which makes recreational use of the latter a punishable offence. To all intents and purposes, alcohol and tobacco are quite definitely mind-altering substances and therefore 'drugs', yet psychologically they are not; we simply do not think of them as drugs in the same way as, for example, heroin or cocaine. This distinction between what we regard as the *real* drugs and the *pretend* drugs is not to be removed by the insistence that they are all drugs. As a consequence, while we are quite happy to distinguish between the non-problem use of alcohol and its abuse, we do not apply the same criterion to illicit drugs. To use heroin or cocaine is to abuse it and the notion of normal or 'social' drug use cannot even be contemplated; the idea that we can talk about heroin or cocaine use in the same way as we refer to alcohol use is basically unthinkable.

Consequently, the word 'drugs' is used primarily to denote a group of substances which we can only conceive of as being abused, and with respect to which the notion of controlled and functional recreational use cannot possibly be entertained. No other single-level distinction differentiates between tobacco and alcohol on the one hand, and 'the drugs of abuse' on the other. It goes without saying, however, that individuals can, and do, regularly experience problems with substances in both categories.

TWO STEREOTYPES

For many people, mention of drug problems conjures up images of the helpless junkie, and a life style characterized by personal neglect, hopelessness, crime, violence, sickness and death. The junkie image is typically one of a person without prospects, without personal pride, without morals, whose every act is dictated by the need to secure further supplies of the precious drug, without which excruciating withdrawal symptoms will inevitably follow. To avoid these terrible symptoms the junkie will do literally anything to obtain the drug he or she craves, so that in some sense the drug takes over the person's very soul and becomes the single motivator for all behaviour. Such a picture is presented in popular fictional accounts of drug use, as in the movie *The French Connection*, or the popular novel *Junkie* by William Burroughs. Such an extreme picture of drug use is, fortunately, not typical. It is indeed a matter for debate as to whether such a stereotype is ever justified. But where do such extreme impressions originate?

The use of illicit drugs such as cannabis, heroin, cocaine, or the currently popular amphetamine derivatives like ecstasy is by definition illegal. Furthermore, the length and frequency of gaol sentences for offences involving the intention to 'supply' (i.e. to sell drugs to others) have increased dramatically over the last ten years, mainly as a result of political pressure (Haw, 1989). This applies to Class B drugs like cannabis, which are generally regarded as being less harmful, as well as to the notorious Class A drugs like heroin and cocaine. Consequently, no one who uses illegal drugs is very keen to identify themselves or allow their drug use to become commonplace knowledge – unless they have no choice or are seeking notoriety through dramatic anonymous interviews with the media. Certainly they are not going to indulge their habit openly in a climate where such behaviour is likely to result in prosecution. Because of this illegal status the public image of the drug user is based for the most part, therefore, on people whose drug use has come into the open for various non-intended reasons: for instance, users who are known to clinics or hospitals in connection with health problems, or to legal and social agencies in connection with theft or family difficulties, that is, a group of people whose drug use has resulted in problems of one kind or another.

If there exists a body of drug users who experience few problems with their habit, they will certainly not broadcast the fact from the rooftops, and their very presence will go largely ignored unless we specifically set out to locate them. Thus our general impressions of drug use will be based on a highly atypical group who encounter serious problems, but these impressions will be no more representative of 'normal' drug use than the stereotype of the 'helpless alcoholic' represents the average social drinker. In fact research from a number of sources (Stimson and Oppenheimer, 1982; Cohen, 1989) reveals that there are many more drug users than come to light through the customary channels. Furthermore, a considerable number of users maintain a controlled pattern of use over long periods of time, work in a steady job, and take care of their families. Yet despite the incontrovertible fact that drug use is typically a very much less dramatic affair than that presented by the junkie stereotype, it is exactly this stereotype which is repeatedly presented in the media. A person who takes drugs and experiences no adverse consequences is hardly front-page news.

A drug problem, therefore, is a problem encountered by someone who takes drugs, and in the interests of common sense we also have to postulate that the problem is in some way related to the person's drug consumption. However, legal considerations apart, there is no inevitable conjunction between taking drugs and experiencing problems. Taking drugs in itself does not necessitate having a drug problem, any more than drinking implies having a drink problem. Therefore, the stereotype of the helpless junkie has only a constrained applicability to a small subset of those who use or have used drugs.

Another stereotypical figure inhabits the twilight world of illicit drugs – namely, the 'evil pusher'. This figure is so unimaginably corrupt that many people would probably endorse the opinion that the death sentence is too good a fate for such a person. Lurking outside the primary school bearing bags of Gummy Bears laced with heroin or cocaine, they lure our very children into a life of chemical dependence and withdrawal symptoms at a time when most of them are still struggling with their three-times table.

The story is a popular one, and many good yarns revolve around this basic plot, in which innocence and youth are enslaved against their will by magical powers wielded by evil agents. After all, we have been brought up on fairytales: the Pied Piper of Hamelin, who wipes out a whole generation of children, compelling them to follow him into his underground discothèque by playing some type of psychoactive acid-house music; or Snow White, lured from the secure, if somewhat questionable, bosom of the seven dwarfs, fed apples laced with psychoactive substances by an unknown pusher disguised as a street trader, and finally rescued from her fate by the sexual advances of a total stranger whilst she lies unconscious; and of course, the Sleeping Beauty, whose problems with dirty needles require no further comment, and whose rescue, having all the same features as Snow White's, clearly suggests that a multiple offender is involved. The battle between good and evil, in the form of youth and innocence, corrupted by evil forces beyond their capacity to control, lies at the heart of some of our most cherished folk myths. The tale of 'The Helpless Junkie and the Evil Drug Pusher' is simply the most recent manifestation.

In fact the reality is rather more prosaic. A number of recent studies of drug users, both in and out of prison, reveal that at the street level drug users tend to sell drugs to each other; furthermore, that attempting to recruit new users by offering them drugs is seen by most drug users as a very good way of ending up in gaol.

At an international level there are drug barons who organize and profit from the processing and distribution of drugs through multinational networks. These are the real pushers, but they are not lurking on our street corners, and the reality of street-level dealing is a very much lower-key affair, with most of the trade being between users, supplementing their income by trading in the substance they themselves use.

Hence the two key characters in the popular perception of the drug scene are more mythical than real, more fiction than fact. Yet according to the stereotype, the junkie is helpless and cannot control his behaviour, whilst the pusher knows what he is doing and is wicked on purpose. Frequently, they are one and the same person, however, and consequently whether a drug offender gets treated as helpless addict or evil pusher depends on a number of chance variables including behaviour at time of arrest, amount of drugs in one's possession, and the impression formed by the arresting officer at the time.

DEFINING THE PROBLEM

Returning now to the question posed at the beginning of this chapter, it is apparent that the difficulties presented by illicit drug use within our society run deeper than the health problems encountered by certain individuals who use drugs. We have observed that alcohol and tobacco are implicated in far more deaths than are the illicit drugs, though we must also accept that their use is far more widespread. We have seen that the image of the helpless junkie, enslaved by his or her substance of abuse, is a myth of our own creation. And we have observed how at different times and in different places various substances we currently regard with alarm have been widely available, whilst others we view with equanimity have been, and still are, illegal.

It should be clear therefore that, from a logical standpoint, use of a substance is not sufficient in itself to justify the term 'drug problem'. Other things being equal, there is no more justification for equating use of some illicit substance with 'addiction' than there is for equating use of alcohol with 'alcoholism'. Unfortunately, however, other things are not equal, due to the differential status of different substances in the eyes of the law. Use of certain drugs is illegal and, consequently, there are major dangers for young people who use them, arising not so much from the risks of dependence and addiction as from the risks attendant on participation in any activity which is illegal. In other words, youngsters who use illegal drugs regularly are at risk in the same way that youngsters who regularly indulge in other illegal activities are at risk. They are more likely to be exposed to a set of influences and values that run contrary to conventional morality and, in so far as they break the law, they run the risk of receiving the prescribed penalties for such behaviour. So far as young people are concerned it is the social context of illicit drug use which poses the greatest cause for concern. By contrast, problems of addiction and dependence arising from the supposed pharmacological properties of the drug come a poor second.

It should be noted that a majority (roughly 65 per cent) of those in prison for drug offences at the present time were convicted of charges involving cannabis (*Drug Scenes*, 1987), which most authorities now regard as relatively benign. Prison sentences are regularly imposed on people found guilty of 'supply' charges relating to cannabis, and the difference between sentence length for cannabis and the Class A drugs has all but disappeared in Scotland (Haw, 1989). Furthermore, users of 'harder' drugs are frequently in prison for some crime other than supply or possession of the drug in question. The danger of illicit drug use for young people is that their lives may be seriously affected by criminal charges arising even from a relatively insignificant cannabis supply charge; and more especially, if they are involved with the so-called harder drugs, some of them may come into contact with criminal values and expertise unrelated to drug use. For teenagers, therefore, a drug problem is most likely to arise from (a) the more broadly criminal context in which some drug use takes place, and (b) the legal consequences of being caught.

Unfortunately, as has been outlined in the preceding sections, the societal consensus on drug addiction is based on beliefs which are stereotyped and inaccurate. Thus most parents, confronted with a child who is found to be using illegal drugs, become hysterical about the possibilities of addiction and death, whereas in fact they should be more concerned about the context in which the drugs are possibly being used, and about the consequences for their son or daughter of being labelled a drug user.

The question of why so many stereotyped and less-than-accurate beliefs surround drug use and drug users is a difficult one, and we shall address those issues in Chapter 3. Before proceeding in that direction, however, it is instructive to look at the magnitude of the drug problem that faces us in order to obtain a better perspective on how drug problems compare with other pressing social problems at the present time. To do this, a number of recent prevalence studies are considered in the chapter that follows, together with some comments on the strengths and weaknesses of such studies.

SUMMARY

Chapter 1 has outlined the very real problems that are caused by the misuse of drugs and pointed to the marked increase in illicit drug use over the last two decades. More people are experiencing drug-related problems than at any other time in our history, and drugs of many kinds are more freely available than ever before. At present, all the signs suggest that use of illicit drugs is likely to increase rather than decrease.

However, an attempt has been made to put these facts into perspective, comparing drug problems with other health risks. It was pointed out that drug users who are not currently encountering health, legal or other problems have no incentive to make their use widely known, and that those who do appear in the public eye tend to have fallen foul of drugs in one way or another, and consequently represent an extreme group.

Stereotyped beliefs about the helpless junkie and the evil pusher were highlighted, and suggestions made as to ways in which these perceptions are oversimplified or inaccurate. The immediate danger for young people lies not so much in the likelihood of their becoming hopeless addicts as in the danger that they will become involved in illegal activities related to drug use which have serious legal and social consequences.

2

HOW PREVALENT IS DRUG USE AMONGST YOUNG PEOPLE?

MEASURING PREVALENCE

Few readers will be surprised to learn that, despite the claims of some social scientists that their methods are beyond scientific reproach, people's answers to survey questions are not always reliable and accurate. There is a large body of research evidence attesting to the fact that answers to questions are often variable and context dependent, varying according to who is asking the questions and why; furthermore, some types of questions and questioning are more likely to lead to misleading information than others. In particular, when people are asked to explain their behaviour or answer questions involving the word *Why?*, their answers are frequently affected by the need to present themselves in a positive light. As we shall see in the next chapter, questions prefaced with 'why' are particularly likely to produce answers which 'make sense' rather than being literally true, and there is a body of psychological theory called 'attribution theory' which addresses this very issue.

Unfortunately, prevalence data on smoking, alcohol use and drug taking cannot realistically be obtained at the present time other than by asking questions and carrying out surveys. Within a free society, there is a limit to how far we can go in order to investigate how people live. We cannot spy on people without their knowledge, or force people to reveal aspects of their lives they may wish to keep to themselves, and so the survey seems the only means available of obtaining the required information. Consequently, when viewing prevalence data, one must always be aware that the method is less than perfect.

None the less, useful information can emerge from prevalence studies if they are properly carried out and if the limitations of the data are acknowledged. They can be carried out in ways which are reliable and replicable; that is, a good study might reasonably be expected to produce the same results if repeated within a reasonable time scale. And when large numbers of people report behaving in a particular way, it can be concluded that this is probably a common behaviour, even if we are less confident about small percentage differences between different groups of people. With respect to drug use, the results from surveys show points of agreement with regard to prevalence, so one can have some confidence in these general findings. On certain topics, survey data are the only data available despite their limitations, and it seems foolish not to make cautious use of what is available. In the remainder of this chapter, therefore, a selection of studies is reviewed. Some of the shortcomings are explained, followed by suggestions as to what may be concluded, and what questions remain unanswered.

WHAT DOES PREVALENCE MEAN?

In the last chapter we saw that the nature of drug use is not accurately reflected by the simple stereotypes that abound. Notwithstanding such oversimplified and polarized beliefs, however, one would think that it was at least possible to know with some certainty *how many* drug users there are. But not surprisingly, assessing the extent of a behaviour that is illegal is not straightforward. For a variety of reasons people who use drugs may not be willing to come forward and say so. There are many reasons why they may not want their families, acquaintances, employers and so forth to know that they use drugs, and so they will be unlikely to reveal their behaviour to open scrutiny.

On the other hand, the stereotype has its uses for drug users whose habit has created legal, social or health problems, and who consequently find themselves in the public eye. In this case, it is functional to present oneself as the 'helpless addict', to report more severe problems, greater dependence and heavier use, and this in fact is what happens (Davies and Baker, 1987). None the less, despite a number of fundamental problems associated with prevalence studies – to be discussed later – there remains a strong interest in the extent of people's involvement with drugs.

The prevalence of drug use is the *frequency* with which it happens in the population. However, drug use is not an-all-or-nothing phenomenon; it can take many different forms. Firstly, there are many different kinds of drugs available: legal and illegal drugs; so-called 'hard' and 'soft' drugs; drugs that stimulate and drugs that depress the central nervous system; hallucinogenic drugs; drugs that cause more or less physiological harm, and so on. Secondly, some people use drugs rarely while others use drugs frequently and this applies to all drugs, legal and illegal, soft and hard.

When faced with a 'shock' media report to the effect that, say, one in five young people have tried or experimented with drugs, it is important to look beyond the statement to determine exactly what it means. It certainly does not mean that one in five young people are regular drug users, much less addicts or junkies. More likely it probably means that one in five young people have tried an illegal drug once or twice, that the drug was probably cannabis, and that no negative consequences arose from the experience. It is not going too far to say that most young people who *try* an illegal drug once or even a few times will almost certainly not adopt use of that drug as a regular part of their behaviour. In order to make sense of drug prevalence statistics it is necessary to ask *which* particular drugs are being referred to and *how often* people are taking them. Only then can one assess the extent to which an apparent problem is a real one.

An often-quoted source of figures is the Home Office annual *Statistical Bulletins*, summarizing two different sorts of relevant data which shed some light on the extent of illegal drug use. These are

(a) statistics on numbers of drug addicts notified to the
UK Home Office;
(b) statistics on the misuse of drugs: seizures and
offenders dealt with in the UK.

The figures revealed in these Home Office reports are derived from notifications from GPs, Drug Dependency Units (DDUs) and other statutory bodies, who are required by law to make notifications under the Misuse of Drugs (Notifications of and Supply to Addicts) Regulations 1973. Doctors notify the Chief Medical Officer at the Home Office with details of people (i.e. patients) believed to be addicted to any of fourteen controlled drugs, including heroin, opium and cocaine. Obviously, the number of 'addicts' notified in this way will be only a proportion of the total number of all those who use, say, heroin or cocaine, and so various 'guesstimates' are produced of the actual number of people who are either addicted to or use such drugs in the population as a whole. For example, *The Guardian* (20 March 1990) reported the Home Office Minister responsible for drugs, David Mellor, asserting that while the recorded total for 'new and renotified addicts for all drugs' had increased to 15,000, the true number of regular drug users would be between 75,000 and 150,000. Doubtless the true total number of regular drug users is in excess of the number notified to the Home Office, but the actual number can only be estimated and even the experts disagree fundamentally, with some suggesting that the real number is up to ten times the known number. However, the basis for adopting a multiplier of ten, or any other number, is at best uncertain and at worst little short of reading sheep's entrails.

That government estimates of prevalence can sometimes be wrong is evidenced by the recent disbanding of a 24-strong joint police and customs task force after less than a year in operation. During its existence this task force, set up to tackle the predicted crack menace, charged only 27 people and seized 13 kilograms of cocaine. Very little crack was found.

While estimates can be wrong, the basis upon which they are made is contained in the Home Office *Statistical Bulletins*, which annually record the number of addicts reported by GPs, hospitals and prison medical officers. In 1989 the number of 'drug addicts' notified to the Home Office increased from 12,644 in 1988 to 14,785, an increase of 2141 or 17 per cent. Of this total, heroin continued to be the most prevalent drug. The number reported as addicted to cocaine only increased a little from 786 (1988) to 888 (1989). It is worth noting that the number of people reported as addicted to cocaine remains a small proportion of total notifications, a fact recognized by the Home Office *Statistical Bulletin* as evidence that misuse of cocaine had not 'so far resulted in significant demands for medical treatment' (*Home Office Statistical Bulletin*, 7/90). This is despite seizures of cocaine that exceeded seizures of heroin by weight between 1987 and 1989.

Another aspect of prevalence is to look at the numbers of seizures and drug offenders dealt with by the police and courts. These data are particularly interesting for the additional light they shed when the totals are broken down by different drugs, something that is not usually done in media reports. In 1988 the total number of seizures (of variable size) in the UK was 38,200. The total was up by 25 per cent on 1987, although the number had remained fairly constant between 1985 and 1987: on the face of it there was a dramatic increase between 1987 and 1989. However, over 88 per cent of these seizures were of cannabis, which is generally considered substantially less serious than heroin or other Class A drugs. So 6,000 of the total number of seizures were for drugs other than cannabis. Thus, if the cannabis figures are taken out of the equation, the statistics look rather less alarming. Of course, it is arguable whether cannabis should be excluded, but the fact remains that, if we talk of soft and hard drugs, it makes sense to be aware of the distinction when examining bald statistics and to attempt to look behind the figures. Whilst it is important to count cannabis and any other drug seizures, there are certain crucial distinctions which should be acknowledged in reports. Although the Home Office statistical bulletin makes this quite clear, the distinction is invariably lost in media reports, to the detriment of better general understanding.

The number of *drug offenders* was 38,400 in 1989, a rise of 25 per cent over the 1988 figure. However, this figure is not a good indication of how many drug users there are *in total*, since it is only possible to make inferences as to what the appropriate multiplier might be. Furthermore, the statistic once again includes a very high proportion who were convicted on cannabis charges. Of the 1989 figure 88 per cent relates to cannabis, 30 per cent up on the previous year, and the highest cannabis figure ever recorded. Given that even the police recognize the greater relative importance of targeting hard drugs it is surprising that so much time and money is devoted to convicting people for cannabis offences.

COUNTING HEADS OR ASSESSING THE PROBLEM?

The Home Office figures for the number of known or 'notified' users are helpful, but only as an indication of the number of drug users in treatment. The figures do not tell us much about drug use in broader terms, and especially not about the extent of drug-related harm at the level of the individual user or in society at large. They do not even tell us whether the individuals notified came to the attention of the doctor *because* of their drug use or for some other reason. In other words, we have to assume that the 15,000 notifications represent a group who were suffering from various sorts of drug-related problems, but the figures provide no guide as to the number or type of problems. The nature of these problems would certainly vary. For instance, some would have said they simply wanted to stop using drugs; some would have suffered physiological harm as a result of unhygienic drug-use practices or through toxic adulteration of their drugs; others may have contacted their doctor as a way of signalling good intentions in the light of a pending prosecution, and so on. This leaves us in the position of not knowing how many of the 15,000 notifications represent people who have real health problems arising from the misuse of drugs *per se*, how many simply want to stop, and how many have problems arising from unsafe drugs or unhygienic drug-use practices. It is therefore impossible, on the basis of these data, to form an accurate impression of the people in question, the nature and severity of their situation, or indeed how many of them have difficulties directly arising from excessive use of some substance.

When we start to examine what is meant by drug problems, we find different categories that could be defined as drug-related: for instance, the problems associated with taking drugs and those that arise because of the way society responds to drug use. Examples of the former include physiological problems caused by using infected needles or drugs adulterated with toxic substances. Examples of the latter include the very illegality of drugs and the stigmatizing of known users and ex-users. Drug-related problems, therefore, come in a variety of forms, and we must be aware that there is more to 'drug problems' than drugs. It is this area, of *understanding* drug-related problems so as to *reduce* them, that is not addressed by straightforward prevalence data.

It is unfortunate that much of the research in drugs and addiction has focused simply on prevalence, albeit often qualified with demographic and socio-economic data. Given that there are more important questions, then estimating the number of people who use drugs is only of limited value in formulating local or national responses. If it were simply the case that all users of certain drugs would necessarily suffer harm as a result, then prevalence data would at least provide concrete evidence of the numbers of people with drug problems known to doctors. But of the drug users not known to doctors or other agencies, the evidence suggests that many of these will *not* have suffered drug-related harm, significant or otherwise. Thus counting heads does not tell us much about the nature of drug problems, nor provide ideas about how best they may be tackled. The *proportion* of drug users who have encountered problems has not been quantified: this may be a large, or only a small, proportion of all users.

COMMUNITY- AND SCHOOL-BASED PREVALENCE STUDIES

The Home Office is only one source of prevalence data. Many studies have focused on samples of people drawn from various communities and a number of studies have been carried out on samples of school pupils. Generally these data are reassuring, in that low rates of regular use are revealed. Overall, about one in five adolescents report having tried an illegal drug at some time (Coggans *et al.*, 1990; Swadi, 1988), but for most of them, this is as far as their experimentation goes. Some adolescents do go on to experiment with other drugs, a few become users on an occasional basis and fewer still become frequent users. Those who proceed to everyday, or nearly everyday, use constitute a very small proportion of the total teenage population. However, we know that the incidence of drug use is not spread evenly throughout the whole population. Drug use is much more common among some groups and in certain localities than in others. There are also differences in the actual drugs preferred by different groups.

A number of prevalence studies have been carried out on samples that are more or less representative of the population as a whole. Briefly, if a study is based on a 'representative' sample then researchers are stating that their sample reflects the characteristics of a particular population. Consequently, what happens in the sample is assumed to be what happens in the population, so the sample *represents* a larger population. Thus, with young people, a representative sample would require to reflect the characteristics to be found amongst young people generally. It would need to include the same range of social and economic backgrounds, the same proportion of males and females, the same age distribution, and so on. The important thing to remember when reading the results of a prevalence study is the validity of generalizing from the sample studied to the population it is supposed to represent. In plainer language, it would be wrong to say that the results of a research study apply to everyone if the study was not based on a representative sample of people.

Prevalence studies can be categorized as general population studies, which look at drug use in representative samples of the whole population, or studies which focus specifically on certain geographical areas or on certain kinds of drug users to find out what is typical behaviour for that specific group. It should not be thought that there is one best way to proceed because different types of study provide different information. For instance, general population studies tell us how prevalent drug use is within the population sampled, while the latter type of study reveals more detail about the drug-using practices of certain groups.

So what do prevalence studies reveal about the extent of drug use? Several studies based on samples of young people allow reasonably accurate judgements to be made as to the proportion of young people who use drugs, both legal and illegal. Most of the prevalence studies

that are based on representative – in some cases *roughly* representative – samples have taken young people as their focus. As would be
expected 'young people' means slightly different things to different
researchers. However, such slight differences in the age range of the
young people surveyed are relatively unimportant for the purposes of
assessing the extent of drug use among adolescents and young adults.

The most recent large-scale prevalence data were collected during
the national evaluation of drug education in Scotland (Coggans *et al.*,
1990). Although the main focus of this study was to assess the effectiveness of drug education in secondary schools, data were also
collected from 1,197 young people on their use of legal and illegal
drugs. (The outcome of this evaluation is discussed in more detail in
Chapter 4.) The young people in this study were all in the second (S2),
third (S3) or fourth (S4) year of their secondary school careers, and
were identified as representative of the range both of social class and
drug education experience typifying Scottish school pupils in S2 to S4
in general.

Participating pupils completed self-report schedules which examined the various drugs used, if any, and the extent of their use. In
addition to alcohol, tobacco, solvents and a list of illegal drugs, pupils
were given the opportunity to report use of any illegal drugs not
covered in the list provided. Pupils who had used any drugs showed
how often they had taken each one by ticking a frequency scale which
ranged from 'never' through to 'every day'. Self-report schedules,
completed anonymously and in confidence, are considered the best
way to assess the extent of drug use in large samples. In addition, the
data collected in this way during the evaluation of drug education
were found to be highly reliable when the same questions were asked
on two different occasions. The details of how this reliability check
was carried out are reported elsewhere (Coggans *et al.*, 1990).

Overall, use of illegal drugs was not found to be extensive. By far the
most frequently used drug was alcohol followed by tobacco, with
cannabis and solvents some way behind, and a range of other drugs
being used on a small scale. Table 2.1 provides a summary of the
percentage of S2 to S4 pupils who reported having taken drugs *at least
once*.

Bearing in mind what was said earlier about the interpretation of
data, it is appropriate to define exactly what these figures tell us. They
merely tell us the percentage of young people (S2 to S4) who have
taken alcohol, tobacco, etc., 'at least once'. In other words there is no
distinction between people who experimented once and those who

Table 2.1. Percentages of young people in a representative sample who have used different drugs at least once

	Drug	Percentage
1.	Alcohol	74
2.	Tobacco	36
3.	Cannabis	15
4.	Solvents	12
5.	Magic mushrooms	7
6.	Temazepam	6
7.	LSD	6
8.	Amphetamine	4
9.	DF118s	2
10.	Barbiturates	2
11.	Temgesic	1
12.	Cocaine	1
13.	Heroin	1
14.	Ecstasy	<1
15.	Crack	<1
16.	Diconal	<1
17.	Other drugs	2

use regularly. Consequently, when we look at a breakdown of the frequency with which young people drink alcohol or smoke cannabis, we find that the number who do so regularly is substantially less than the number who report having tried these things 'at least once' or 'on a few occasions' or whatever.

The examples detailed in the separate sections below, headed *alcohol*, *tobacco*, *illegal drugs* and *solvents*, will suffice to highlight this point.

Table 2.2. Frequency of use: alcohol

Category response	Percentage	Actual number
Never	26.2	315
Only once	16.4	197
A few times	31.1	373
Sometimes, but less than once a month	8.8	106
About once a month	8.1	97
About once a week	8.1	97
Nearly every day	0.4	5
Every day	0.2	2
Total		1192

Alcohol

From Table 2.2 it can be seen that most had drunk alcohol a few times, while those who could be defined as regular drinkers (once a month or once a week) comprised about 16 per cent. The proportion who reported drinking every day or nearly every day was less than 1 per cent. The rate of at-least-once for alcohol has been assessed as 74 per cent amongst 13- to 16-year-olds (Coggans *et al.*, 1990), 63 per cent amongst 11- to 16-year-olds (Swadi, 1988) and 98 per cent of 15- and 16-year-olds (Plant, Peck and Stuart, 1982). Despite the similarity of these figures – older pupils were more likely to have drunk alcohol than younger pupils – the proportion who have had alcohol once is of marginal importance given that drinking once is probably not in itself a problem. When we look at the proportion who reported drinking more frequently we find that 16.8 per cent reported drinking 'about once a month' or more frequently. Fewer pupils, 8 per cent, reported drinking 'about once a week', while less than 1 per cent reported drinking 'every day' or 'nearly every day'. Swadi (1988) found that 11.6 per cent of his sample reported drinking 'once or more than once a week', a figure that is broadly similar to the national evaluation of drug education data (9.7 per cent).

The likelihood of drinking alcohol was not influenced by drug education, sex or social class. It was, however, influenced by age so that older adolescents were more likely to drink than younger adolescents.

Tobacco

Table 2.3 shows the frequency breakdown for tobacco. Nearly one in five young adolescents smoked infrequently, and 18.8 per cent reported smoking less than once a month, while 2.4 per cent reported smoking about once a week or about once a month. However, 14 per cent smoked cigarettes every day or nearly every day. Interestingly, cigarette smoking was the one form of drug use that showed what is known technically as bimodal distribution of frequency, or in plain language two apparently distinct groups of smokers. One sizeable group smoked very infrequently (18.8 per cent), while another group (14 per cent) were frequent smokers. Infrequent and frequent in this context is not quite the same as heavy and light smokers, as the actual number of cigarettes smoked during each smoking episode was not recorded.

Cigarette smoking was more likely if the young people concerned

Table 2.3. Frequency of use: tobacco

Category response	Percentage	Actual number
Never	64.1	769
Only once	6.7	87
A few times	10.1	121
Sometimes, but less than once a month	2.0	24
About once a month	1.1	13
About once a week	1.3	15
Nearly every day	3.9	47
Every day	10.0	120
Total		1196

were older, female and from lower socio-economic groups than if they were younger, male and from higher socio-economic backgrounds. While the fact that older adolescents are more likely to smoke than younger ones may not be particularly surprising, and similarly that a lower socio-economic background is associated with a greater likelihood of smoking, it might surprise some readers to discover that girls are more likely to smoke than boys. None the less, this sex-related finding accords with a trend that has been evident for a number of years. Evidence from the early 1980s showed that girls had caught up with boys in their rates of smoking (Kandel, 1980; Bachman, Johnston and O'Malley, 1981; Sheppard, 1984). Now it appears that while more girls are smoking, fewer boys are doing so, and that overall prevalence remains the same (Swadi, 1988). Despite these findings in terms of prevalence, the causal contribution of age, sex and social class to adolescent smoking was relatively minimal, as analysis of the relationship between these background factors and rates of smoking has shown (Coggans *et al.*, 1990). The role of individual characteristics such as personal beliefs about the costs and benefits of smoking will probably be a more significant factor in whether young people become smokers or not.

Illegal drugs and solvents

Three examples from the list of illegal drugs (namely cannabis, heroin and cocaine) clearly indicate that use of illegal drugs, particularly the so-called hard drugs, occurs on a small scale (see Tables 2.4 to 2.7). Even cannabis is smoked regularly by only a small percentage in this age group, with most use being occasional. Heroin use was reported by less than 1 per cent, as was cocaine use.

Table 2.4. Frequency of use: cannabis

Category response	Percentage	Actual number
Never	85.3	980
Only once	5.0	57
A few times	6.2	71
Sometimes, but less than once a month	1.0	11
About once a month	0.6	7
About once a week	1.2	14
Nearly every day	0.3	4
Every day	0.2	2
Total		1146

Table 2.5. Frequency of use: heroin

Category response	Percentage	Actual number
Never	99.2	1136
Only once	0.5	6
A few times	0.3	3
Total		1145

Table 2.6. Frequency of use: cocaine

Category response	Percentage	Actual number
Never	99.2	1136
Only once	0.3	4
A few times	0.3	3
Sometimes, but less than once a month	0.2	2
Total		1145

Data of this sort are reassuring for parents worried about the probability of their children taking drugs, but it should be said that this low level of probability is not evenly spread throughout society. Drug use varies between groups in society, so that young people in some areas would be more likely to come into contact with drugs than those in other areas. While local variations do exist, it would be erroneous to assume that use of illegal drugs is related in a simple fashion to social class. Although it was found that a lower social class background was associated with greater likelihood of using illegal drugs, it must be noted that the influence of this background factor is slight. Personal beliefs about the advantages and disadvantages of using drugs are more likely to be important in predicting drug use. However, it cannot be assumed that young people perceive the costs and benefits in the same terms as many adults do. For instance, many adults believe that there are no benefits and only costs associated with drug use; yet people who take drugs frequently perceive benefits. What this means is that the importance of personal beliefs about the costs or benefits of drug use and the development of such beliefs is likely to be a fruitful focus for research into the causes of drug use.

A recent study carried out in London comprehensive schools found that the prevalence rate of 'ever' use of illegal drugs or solvents increased from 13 per cent amongst 11-year-olds to 26 per cent in 16-year-olds and the prevalence rate of repeated use (defined as 'daily' or 'occasional' use) increased from 2 per cent of 11-year-olds to 16 per cent of 16-year-olds (Swadi, 1988). Interestingly, Swadi found that substance use increased sharply between 11 and 14 years but thereafter there was an insignificant increase in use between 14 and 16 years. However, not all studies produce identical results, and not all studies are easily compared. For example, depending on which prevalence study is examined, cannabis has been tried by 11 per cent (approximately) of 11- to 16-year-olds (Swadi, 1988), 15 per cent of 13- to 16-year-olds (Coggans *et al.*, 1990), and 7 per cent of 15- to 16-year-olds (Plant, Peck and Samuel, 1985).

However, experimentation or very occasional use, in itself, is of less concern than more frequent use. Table 2.4 shows the breakdown of cannabis use in the sample who participated in the evaluation of drug education referred to earlier (Coggans *et al.*, 1990). If we take 'about once a month' and more frequent use as the definition of regular use, and the lower frequencies as occasional use, then there were 2.3 per cent regular users and 12.2 per cent occasional users. If we look only at those who smoke cannabis every day or nearly every day, the proportion goes down to 0.5 per cent. It would appear, then, that the prevalence of regular use, and use 'most days' in particular, is very low in a cross-section of adolescents. In addition, these data do not address the *amount* smoked on any one occasion. So it is quite possible that the proportion of adolescents who smoke cannabis heavily every day is rather low.

Fourth most prevalent after alcohol, tobacco and cannabis (see Table 2.1) were solvents, which had been used by 10.9 per cent of the sample at least once, though only 0.7 per cent reported using once a

Table 2.7. Use of solvents

Frequency	Percentage	Actual number
Never	87.6	1051
Only once	5.8	70
A few times	4.1	49
Sometimes, but less than once a month	0.3	4
About once a month	0.3	3
About once a week	0.2	2
Every day	0.2	2
Total		1181

month or more frequently. Most of those who had used solvents had used them only once or a few times (see Table 2.7).

The remaining illegal drugs are only used by a small (in some cases tiny) percentage of adolescents. It may come as a surprise to some people that drugs such as heroin, for example, are used only by a small proportion of the general population. A great deal of publicity has been given to heroin and other hard drugs over recent years, even though other drugs such as alcohol and tobacco are responsible for vastly greater harm. Heroin is a good example of a drug whose consumption could be thought to have reached epidemic proportions, if government posters and media reports – *stories* is a more accurate term in many cases – were one's only source of information. In overall terms heroin is used by less than 1 per cent of adolescents (Coggans *et al.*, 1990) or by less than 2 per cent (Swadi, 1988). None the less, heroin was the subject of many prevention campaigns in the 1980s, especially 'fear-arousal' campaigns, a fact that was commented on by different researchers. They felt that emphasis in these campaigns on heroin was misplaced, given the much greater prevalence of other drugs, alcohol and tobacco in particular (Bagnall and Plant, 1988; Swadi, *op. cit.*). Fear arousal in the context of information about drugs means the sort of posters or advertisements that are intended to shock or to frighten. It is interesting to note that the government's own advisory body, the Advisory Council on the Misuse of Drugs (ACMD), took the view in their report on prevention in 1984 that 'Drug education should not concentrate solely on factual information about drug misuse, *even less present such information in a way that is intended to shock or scare*' (emphasis added).

While media campaigns which focused specifically on heroin using the fear-arousal approach appear to have become largely a thing of the past (at the time of writing), the fear-arousal approach itself is still evident in the most recent government-funded anti-drugs media campaign ('Drugs – the effects can last for ever'), launched in the spring of 1990. Although non-specific in terms of actual drugs, this campaign is very firmly within the fear-arousal category. Furthermore, despite the advice of the ACMD, the then Prime Minister, Margaret Thatcher, at the World Ministerial Drug Summit in London in April 1990, made clear her preference for even more of this sort of advertising. It seems that we can expect more fear-arousal anti-drugs campaigns, despite the evidence that fear arousal can be counter-productive (de Haes and Schuurman, 1975; Schaps *et al.*, 1981) and the advice of the government's own expert advisers that such an approach should not be employed.

Drug education is dealt with in more detail in Chapter 4. The purpose of this short digression is to highlight the impact that anti-drug campaigns have on how the public perceive the problem. Dramatic and shocking posters depicting the worst possible consequences, which do not happen to all or even most heroin users, serve only to inflate negative perceptions amongst the non-heroin-using population with the result that people come to believe that, say, heroin causes more deaths than alcohol. However, we know that alcohol is responsible for roughly 30 times more deaths than heroin. The question remains, then, as to why the government prefers such tactics for heroin and not for alcohol: an issue beyond the scope of this chapter.

Taking all the prevalence data together – legal and illegal drugs – the most striking thing is that alcohol and tobacco are the most commonly used drugs. At the level of experimentation, alcohol is by far the most prevalent drug, having been tried by more than seven out of ten adolescents. While it is going too far to say that such a high level of experimentation is itself a problem, it is not going too far to say that this experimenting rate is indicative of a drug that is widely available – and legally available within certain restrictions. Availability is doubtless a major factor in whether any drug is tried or used regularly. Far fewer young people have experimented with tobacco (36 per cent) than with alcohol, but 10 per cent reported smoking every day and a further 4 per cent reported smoking 'nearly every day'. In other words, 14 per cent of young people are regular smokers. Of all the drugs taken by young people, then, tobacco is the most serious from a number of perspectives. First, a very high proportion (41 per cent) of those who have tried tobacco reported smoking every or nearly every day. In comparison, of those who have tried cannabis only 3 per cent report every-day or nearly every-day consumption. Second, because of its widespread use, cigarette smoking is hazardous to public health, through damage to the lungs in particular. Third, very high levels of harmful cigarette use can be incorporated into one's daily routine with relatively few restrictions on consumption. There are few major social impediments to smoking once the habit is established, and even harmful levels are accepted by the society in which we live. This means that social pressures of the type experienced by illicit drug users are not present for the majority of smokers.

Finally, if the 'slippery slope' theory of drug use – that once you start with soft drugs you inevitably progress to more frequent use and on to hard drugs – is valid, then we would expect to see certain consequences. First, we would expect a far higher percentage of *regular* users amongst those who report having smoked cannabis. Second, given the level of cannabis smoking reported amongst the sample, we might expect to find a higher percentage of use or even experimentation with heroin. These data do not support the 'slippery slope' theory. While it is possible to demonstrate that people who use heroin may also have smoked cannabis at some time, that is not evidence that cannabis leads to heroin. On the contrary, there are many people who have smoked cannabis who have not even tried other illegal drugs, far less 'progressed' to heroin.

SUMMARY

Chapter 2 has addressed the problems of measuring prevalence. The nature of prevalence data was discussed, and the purposes which such data can meaningfully serve, as well as their weaknesses. The reader was cautioned about the kinds of inferences which may or may not be made on the basis of prevalence data and was encouraged to take a critical view of survey data wherever easy conclusions appear to be drawn. The need to be aware of the *exact basis on which the data were collected* was stressed.

With respect to young people, whilst there is clear cause for concern, there is no reason for extreme pessimism. Although the studies cited reveal that experience with illicit drugs is quite widespread, with perhaps one in five schoolchildren having taken an illicit substance at some time, it is equally clear that the numbers who use such drugs regularly is much smaller, and that the percentage using Class A drugs is a fraction of 1 per cent.

The available evidence also points to the fact that, amongst young people, use of alcohol and cigarettes is far more widespread than use of illegal substances, and there is also more regular use of alcohol and cigarettes. Notwithstanding the generally low levels of regular illicit drug use shown in these studies, it was pointed out that there are regional variations in extent of use of these substances, and use of illicit drugs by young people is without doubt more common in certain deprived inner-city areas than in other locations.

3

MYTHS ABOUT DRUG ADDICTION

In Chapter 1 we examined some of the facts and misconceptions surrounding the illicit use of drugs. Reference was made to the stereotype of the 'helpless junkie' and to the sometimes exaggerated beliefs that people hold about the powers of particular substances. Chapter 2 analysed the findings from a number of recent prevalence studies indicating that whilst a sizeable percentage of young people have experience with an illicit drug, the number who regularly indulge or who have what may be termed a 'drug habit' is very small.

Given the general tone of these findings, one might well ask 'Where do these stereotyped and over-simplified beliefs originate?' and 'What purpose is served by these stereotyped beliefs?' This chapter looks at the role of the media in disseminating particular messages, and some suggestions are made as to why alternative messages appear less regularly. Secondly, the role of research in this process is laid open. The fact that particular kinds of questions can sometimes predispose to particular kinds of answers has already been mentioned. Recent research suggests that when users are asked to explain their drug use, their answers are sometimes self-serving, or else they 'make sense of' the questions being asked, in ways that are not immediately apparent. Certain types of answers appear to be constructed in order to serve various types of social function, and the researcher is in error if he or she assumes that 'truth' is simply and invariably revealed when people are asked to recall events, or to explain why they happened.

DRUG MYTHS IN THE MEDIA

Misconceptions are usually fostered and fuelled by the newspapers, television and other media, for a variety of reasons. There is no doubt that for some media workers, the only contact they have with illicit drug use in the world at large is by way of their own or their colleagues' coverage of the issue. In our experience, it is not difficult to find reporters whose views of addiction accord closely with the general stereotype; small wonder then if they perpetuate misinformation, simply because those who report the news have not been exposed to a message based on a more realistic appraisal of the facts. In such a situation, people unconsciously select and sift the information at their disposal in such a way as to confirm the general wisdom.

There is also the suspicion that some newspapers are primarily driven by economics and that the need to inform is nothing more than a banner of convenience, which can be used as justification when the occasion requires. Within such a context, balanced coverage of difficult issues is almost impossible to envisage; reports of drug use that are less than lurid consequently find no place in an agenda dictated by the need to uncover stories more shocking than those which sold the papers yesterday. Acts of violence or theft by drug users are attributed to the drugs directly; drug-related behaviour is 'drug-crazed' behaviour; drug use is assumed to lead to serious illness and death as a matter of course; and a highly polarized picture of the war between good and evil is presented. To take a single example from the many available, the *Mirror* newspaper of 30 August 1989 could with impunity print a story about Colombian cocaine production, along with photographs of Fabio Ochoa and his sons, under the headline: 'Warning. These men are killing your kids.' In fact, the number of our 'kids' dying from cocaine misuse is extremely small; if by 'kids' we mean those below thirteen years, almost non-existent. In fact, a picture of an average man driving his car down an average street would have done far more justice to the headline than the 'evil Colombian' who was featured in the article in question.

This single example will suffice, without the need for a catalogue of media horrors and accompanying self-righteous rhetoric. However, it is too easy to place all the blame on the popular press, and to ignore the fact that alternative perspectives on drug use do appear from time to time both in the papers and on television, although these may appear to be in a minority. It must also be said that some of the more respected news outlets, including papers like the *Observer* and television programmes like 'Panorama', have also been responsible for perpetuating drug myths; a fact which is perhaps more dangerous since they are more likely to be believed. Thus stories of the substance which enslaves after a single experience and tales of helpless addicts driven to crime by their need for drugs and the agony of withdrawal can be found at all levels in the media and are not the sole territory of the tabloids. Within this general torrent, those rarer presentations which offer a more differentiated and balanced picture tend to go unnoticed.

To a large extent, the media create their own agenda where drugs are concerned. Because of the pervasive nature of the myth, participants in documentary programmes know the required 'script' in general terms, and the programme merely brings to life a message that is implicit from the start. A documentary is not like a piece of research on film. It cannot go wherever the forces of logic compel it, but rather represents a search for visual material to support a story that is there at the inception. Consequently, a programme aimed at highlighting problems of drug abuse will require material that supports that script. Interviews with users who report having no problems or who use drugs because they want to (rather than because they are 'forced' to) will simply not appear. In a sense, therefore, the medium creates its own reality. The danger in this process is that we thereby help to create a drug problem in the image of the media coverage, rather than in terms of an alternative and more dynamic reality.

Furthermore, alternative accounts are readily accessible if one goes about things in a different way, since the manner in which people present themselves is known to vary according to context and circumstance. This variability in self-presentation has been well documented in the research literature, but the fact that the world as revealed in the media differs from the world as revealed elsewhere is seldom taken on board.

When people are asked to give face-to-face accounts of themselves, especially on sensitive issues, it is true to say that the information provided by the interviewee cannot be considered independently of the methods used to obtain it and the circumstances prevailing at the time. This interdependence between the nature of an interview and the material that comes out of it has been well documented, and it is now appropriate to look at some concrete examples.

WHO ASKS THE QUESTIONS?

In the 1960s a series of studies was carried out by Belson, Millerson and Didcott (1968) at the Survey Research Centre in London, which investigated acts of theft by adolescent boys. In addition to their interest in theft, and the ways in which boys from different social backgrounds could commit the same acts but suffer different consequences, Belson *et al.* were also fascinated by the ways in which the interview situation itself affected the accounts that the boys provided. Belson used a range of individual interview methods, from a fairly relaxed face-to-face situation to one in which interviewer and interviewee were separated by a screen and where no casual conversation was permitted before or after. He also experimented with different styles of interviewer, including a more or less formal style and a more 'cool' or 'laid-back' approach. Belson found that the degree and type of self-disclosure depended on the method used. Furthermore, he concluded that it was impossible to say that any method produced more 'truth' than any other and that whilst the data might prove useful in helping to separate those who stole *more* from those who stole *less*, there was no way of determining by these means what the *actual extent* of theft was. The fundamental importance of Belson's studies and similar work by others, which reveals that the data obtained in a face-to-face interview cannot be regarded independently of the method used to obtain them and the apparent purpose of the study, has however been lost sight of. In the place of an empirical and self-critical approach to research methods, we have arrived at a situation where increasing reliance is placed on high but unmeasurable levels of 'trust' and 'understanding' between interviewer and interviewee as the only guarantee that the data are what they seem to be. Certainly, richer data are obtained by 'in-depth' methods, but whether they are 'truer' in some absolute sense is unknown and unknowable. It seems more likely that these methods, like any other, have their own strengths and weaknesses.

Belson's studies, described briefly in the paragraphs above, were used as the basis for an investigation of interviewer bias effects with drug users. In a study by Davies and Baker (1987) twenty heroin users were interviewed on two occasions, separated by a period of between ten and fourteen days. The set of questions used in the interviews had two forms, form 'a' and form 'b'; that is, two 'parallel forms' were produced in which the meaning of the questions was the same, but the precise wording was different. This was to prevent the subjects from realizing that they had been asked the same questions on both occasions. Half of the drug users received interview 'a', followed by interview 'b'; the other half received the interviews in the opposite order. The crucial variable in the study, however, was the person who did the interviewing. Each of the subjects was interviewed on the first occasion by a current heroin user specifically recruited and trained in interviewing techniques, and on the second occasion by a 'straight' interviewer representing the research (ARGUS) group.

The data obtained by the two interviewers were substantially, and in statistical terms significantly, different. When interviewed by the 'straight' interviewer, the users presented themselves as using more drugs, as spending more on drugs, as having to steal more to support the habit, as being more dependent, as having more severe withdrawal symptoms, and as being in greater need of treatment. Importantly, they were also more likely to explain their drug use in terms of internal addiction-type factors (factors implying that they used drugs because of things to do with their physiological state) when interviewed by the 'straight' interviewer. To the drug-using interviewer, however, the picture of use presented was less extreme: less severe symptoms were reported, and the subjects also implied that their use was more a function of external circumstances than of internal physiology. In other words, to some extent they presented themselves differently to each of the two interviewers.

In case the reader is sceptical of these findings, it is worth pointing out that earlier research by Ball (1967) in the United States has shown the same kind of results. Straight interviewers from outside the drug-using culture obtained a more extreme picture from drug users. On this issue it remains only to say that data from drug users are almost always obtained by straight interviewers, and hardly ever by other drug users. As we have seen, this is a method likely to produce a more extreme picture, and that picture is more likely to contain key components of the junkie stereotype.

With respect to the arguments about 'in-depth' interviews and 'trust', one might speculate that the drug user from the midst of the very culture under investigation would have more in-depth knowledge, more credibility, and be more trusted than a 'straight' from a clinic or university. Notwithstanding such speculation, however, the study simply shows that the data obtained vary according to the type of person sent to collect them. From the point of view of this chapter, the news reporter or television crew are simply another group of interviewers from *outside* the drug culture, who will obtain a particular picture of drug use which cannot be divorced from the particular role that the media play in our society.

It is plain to see, therefore, that when data on some sensitive issue such as drug use are collected by asking questions, people's answers can be influenced in a variety of ways, according to what they make of the interview situation. Furthermore, it seems likely that regular or heavy users will frequently be the ones who have the most to lose or gain from particular types of self-presentation. None the less, such self-reports are still frequently taken as indicators of the way the world actually is, rather than the world filtered and interpreted by a thinking human being with motives and intentions, dealing with an interviewer from a different social world who may be potentially threatening, untrustworthy, a possible ally, or whatever. Where such uncertainty exists, a version of events centring on the 'helpless addict' represents the best strategy for the widest range of purposes, eliciting help from the sympathetic listener whilst simultaneously offering the best defence against attack. It is difficult to imagine why a drug user should present any other picture to the public when he or she is confronted by the film camera or the news reporter.

RESEARCH FINDINGS

In the last chapter, we introduced two notions concerning the ways in which people answer questions. Firstly, we suggested that the evidence on verbal reports leads to the conclusion that what people say depends on a variety of situational factors, and that people present themselves differently according to circumstances. This is so obviously correct that the alternative notion, that people present themselves the same way in all situations, seems barely worth considering. The second point extends this observation by suggesting that people's answers to questions are underlaid by functionality; that is, their answers do not merely vary between situations in some random or unpredictable way. Rather, people present themselves differently in different situations *on purpose*, because they have their own good reasons for doing so. Consequently, to the extent that this is true, people's answers to questions are generally a poor guide to the way the world is, and, indeed, 'truth' can never be revealed by these means. On the other hand, their answers might in principle provide a useful insight into the way they see the world, and the functions they therefore wish their answers to serve. In other words, they can reveal things about the ways people think, and that is primarily what people's answers to questions are good at.

In the following paragraphs, we present some research findings which show that whilst drugs users' verbal reports are variable and context dependent, they are indeed functional in nature and 'make sense' of the situation in which the drug user finds himself or herself. More specifically, the bias in their answers reveals that they feel the need to justify their drug use behaviour, to minimize the blame that others will attach to it, and to make the drugs appear to be the primary cause of their problem, whenever they present themselves to the public view. This in turn reveals that they *know* that the broader society will take a moral and punitive view of their actions; hence their defensive strategy. The following sections illustrate the essentially strategic nature of people's answers to questions about their substance use, and how a plausible and coherent picture can emerge which is primarily an act of self-presentation.

What do people remember?

Questions in which subjects are asked to recall past events play an important part in addiction research. Thus, age at which drug use commenced, symptoms experienced and their order of onset, and recollection of distressing or stressful events are key features in certain theoretical models. For example, some research suggests that those encountering serious problems are likely to have started using drugs at an earlier age; recall of the onset of various symptoms can be taken to indicate the extent to which the addiction has progressed; stressful life events are sometimes assumed to be triggers which cause people to turn to drugs, or cause them to relapse if they are trying to give up.

It is important to realize, however, that when people remember things, it is an active process. Memories are acts of cognitive construction, and to a very great extent the things we remember depend on the circumstances we are in and the functions the recollection is intended to serve. Memory is also selective, and major differences exist between prompted and unprompted recall. For example, the open-ended question 'What did you do last week?' will usually produce a totally different picture from that revealed in a forced-choice check-list, in which lots of activities are listed and the subject instructed to 'Tick off the things that you did last week'.

In contrast to this functional, constructionist and dynamic view of memory is the idea that memory is simply a refrigerated storehouse of things that happened. If you ask a 'memory' question, the person goes into the storehouse and either finds the appropriate memory, duly passing it over intact and unadulterated to the experimenter, or else fails to find it, i.e. forgets. Consequently, if you want to know what happened to people and what they did, there is an easy short-cut to finding out. You just ask them, and they either tell you because they have remembered it or they don't because they have forgotten. If they tell you, they must have remembered.

It must be obvious to everyone that the monolithic view of memory outlined above is quite false, and that we reinterpret and refine our memories at every twist and turn, so as to present ourselves in the ways we feel are appropriate to different situations. Sometimes we accentuate or exaggerate, sometimes we gloss over something or underplay it in order to appear modest, or whatever. Furthermore, this is something we all do, not just drug users or some other group who are under scrutiny. It will come as no surprise therefore to find that memory data can often be unreliable in fundamental ways, and that they vary according to the context. The following paragraphs outline some examples from our own experience.

How old were you when you started using?

In 1972, a study by Davies and Stacey was published, which investigated alcohol use by young people. The study, which was based on answers to a questionnaire, asked about young people's experience with, and perception of, alcohol. One of these questions, which occurs in a majority of studies of alcohol and other drug use, asked subjects to recall the age at which they first started drinking. Casual inspection of the data showed that many subjects gave an age which, if traced back, indicated that they started drinking in 1969. This seemed rather odd; there seemed nothing about 1969 that would lead teenagers suddenly to start drinking.

Statistical analysis eventually solved the problem. The sample consisted of youngsters aged between 14 years and 17 years. It became apparent that age of reported first drink was closely associated with (correlated with) the age of the person. So 17-year-olds tended to answer 'Fourteen', 16-year-olds tended to say 'Thirteen' and so on. Everybody, in other words, made some sort of reasoned guess, going back about three years, that is, to 1969. A subsequent study of drinking by 10- to 14-year-olds (Aitken, 1978) included the same question and, once again, reported age of first drink predicted the age of the subject better than it predicted anything else. Finally, in a more recent study (Hammersley *et al.*, 1989) drug use was investigated amongst heroin users both in and out of prison. Once again, we asked subjects to remember the age at which they started using. And once again, with this adult sample, reported age of first drug use predicted how old the respondent was better than it predicted anything else. It is now clear that this question produces reliable and systematic data, but that it does not actually measure what it appears to measure. People are very unclear about the age at which they started doing things; they acquire behaviours over periods of time rather than all at once. Consequently, people provide reasoned but symbolic answers to this question, in order to satisfy the requirements of the interview or questionnaire.

It remains only to say that questions about age of first use are still prominent in drug and alcohol questionnaires of all kinds, and that many other questions are 'regulars' of this type, but their pedigree has not been researched in any detail. The literature on addiction contains a number of discussions about whether earlier use predisposes to later misuse or not. To the extent that it does, we can now see that the apparent relationship between earlier use and later problems may be based on data which are deceptive. It seems entirely feasible that people with drug problems will report earlier use because it seems reasonable to do so, rather than because they have any actual memory of the details. Whatever the truth of the matter, our fear that earlier drug use by children or teenagers will automatically predispose to more serious drug problems later is founded on data which are highly unsatisfactory.

Recalling symptoms

Finally on the topic of memory, a study by Anderson, Aitken and Davies (1981) examined recall of symptoms by a group of problem drinkers. The study derived from earlier work by Chick and Duffy (1979), which showed that a group of people with alcohol problems recalled broadly similar symptoms *and a similar ordering for the onset of those symptoms*, when asked to do so. Basically, a 'check-list' (items were written on cards) type of approach was used in the original study, and the findings were interpreted as having useful implications in diagnosing severity of dependence. In the replication study by Anderson *et al.* (1981) it was again found that the problem drinkers showed a high degree of reliability and consistency in recalling the symptoms they had experienced as their plight deteriorated and also were in substantial agreement about the order in which the symptoms occurred. There was just one problem: a control group of people, screened to eliminate anyone with an alcohol problem, could produce exactly the same results when they were asked to 'pretend they had a drink problem' and then carry out the same task. In other words, in order to do the task satisfactorily, it was not necessary to remember anything at all. In all probability the symptoms listed, and their apparent severity, provide all that is needed for a highly reliable set of results, which are based on common sense rather than on memory.

Is drug use a response to life stress?

A second aspect of memory, namely its 'constructed' nature, was illustrated in a study of stress and drug use. Literature exists on the notion that people use drugs primarily as a response to life stress, as some sort of a crutch to buffer them against misfortune and hardship. A detailed review of this literature exists (O'Doherty and Davies, 1987) which shows plainly that there are serious methodological problems with some of the research in this area.

In its simplest form, work on life stress and substance use consists of (a) asking people to provide information about their substance use over some period of time, followed by (b) asking the same people to recall stressful events and their timing over the same time period. The fact that statistical analysis subsequently shows that the two data sets are associated (correlated) is normally taken as evidence that (b) causes (a). Whilst not all life-events work follows this pattern exactly, many studies have this basic design as their starting point.

One study of particular interest was conducted in the 1950s (Stott, 1958) into the possible relationship between Down's syndrome (so-called 'mongolism') and stress during pregnancy. In a study basically to the above design, Stott found that a sample of mothers of Down's syndrome children reported significantly more life stress during pregnancy than did a matched sample of mothers of normal children. The study is important because, in this instance, subsequent medical research revealed that Down's syndrome was a consequence of chromosomal abnormality, and not therefore a consequence of external events.

The question raised by the study is, 'How does the relationship between Down's syndrome and reports of stressful events come about, when the real pattern of causality lies at a chromosomal level?' The answer is, of course, that the method used in the study leads the people who took part to make their own sense of what is going on. Consequently, a mother of a Down's syndrome child, asked a battery of questions about possible stress during pregnancy, starts to *think*. She does not merely transmit information from the past like some inanimate telephone link, but starts to look for, and to find, events that make sense of the study. Obviously, the doctor believes that stress during pregnancy might have something to do with it, or else he wouldn't be asking the questions. The idea is appealing: the researcher wants his explanation; that explanation is to some extent reasonable and acceptable; small wonder then that researcher and research subject find what they are looking for, i.e. a story that makes acceptable sense of what might be seen as a personal tragedy. Only in this specific case did subsequent research reveal the socially constructed nature of the findings, when an explanation at the chromosomal level was discovered.

In the area of drug use, however, no clear alternative explanation has been revealed, and so research findings derived from the same basic methodology tend to be taken at face value.

In our own study (O'Doherty, 1988; O'Doherty and Davies, 1988), we simply interviewed six groups of people (drug users, problem drinkers and problem smokers, each with their own matched control group) on six occasions over an eighteen-month period, at three-monthly intervals. The details of the study are available elsewhere, but basically subjects were asked to recall stressful events over the last three-month period that had significantly affected them. A pattern of relationships was found between drug use and reports of stressful events that varied according to how one classified the events. But most striking was the appearance of the 'memory' data, which contain a clear artefact. Figures 3.1 to 3.6 reveal two main effects: first, people reported less and less the longer the study went on; more interestingly, all groups reported most stressful events as occurring in the weeks immediately prior to each interview (i.e. months 3, 6, 9, etc.).

The pattern is clearly artefactual; it is most unreasonable to argue that by chance all our subjects experienced real life stresses just before the interview, and that this was true over all six interviews for six groups of people. What is revealed is the fact that people construct accounts of themselves that are influenced by the design of the study, and the reasons for the artefact are not difficult to find. However, the artefact is only revealed because we did the study, in effect, six times.

Once again, however, it must be repeated that the above is nothing new. A paper by Jenkins, Hurst and Rose (1979) specifically addresses the dangers of the 'one-off' life stress study, and the artefactual fall-off in recall. In the meantime, a steady stream of studies continues to emerge showing associations between drug use and verbal reports of life stress, since that is the acceptable reality. The 'inadequacy' model, and the idea that drug use derives only from sets of negative dynamics (from sick people; from atypical or unfortunate circumstances; from

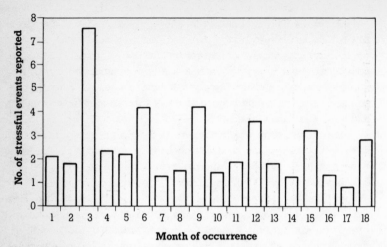

Figure 3.1 Heroin group

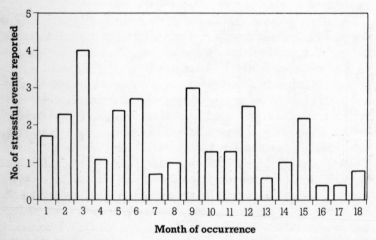

Figure 3.2 Alcohol group

42

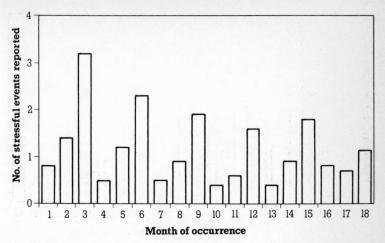

Figure 3.3 Tobacco group

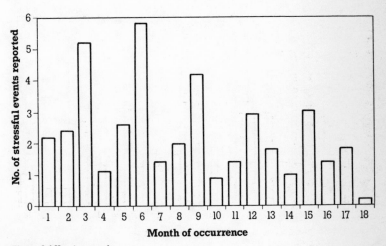

Figure 3.4 Heroin controls

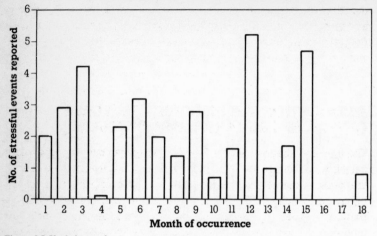

Figure 3.5 Alcohol controls

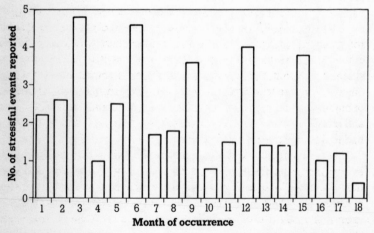

Figure 3.6 Tobacco controls

evil substances), is the one we wish to live with, and we require evidence to support that contention. The methodological adequacy of the research has almost become an irrelevance, because the alternative view, that increasing numbers of perfectly normal and rational people choose to use drugs on purpose, because they like it and they want to, is too threatening to contemplate.

ATTRIBUTION THEORY: ARE ANSWERS TO QUESTIONS PRIMARILY FUNCTIONAL?

The final illustration concerns a body of research into the psychological theory of 'attribution'. One of the facets of this theory, of interest in the present context, is the idea that we offer explanations for our behaviour which are motivated rather than neutral; that is, we choose particular types of explanation because they are functional. This tendency is most marked in the case of questions which begin with the word 'Why?' – 'Why did you do this?' or 'Why did you take that?' – or whatever.

When asked such questions, people naturally enough provide reasons for their actions, but there is a great tendency to confuse such reasons with *causes*. Reasons in this context are psychological constructions and give information as to how the person wishes us to view and interpret the act in question. This can be quite different from the picture revealed when we search for a *cause* in a statistical sense. For example, if we do something good and praiseworthy, we tend to explain it by referring to properties of ourselves. Thus, if we give money to a Third-World charity, we are more likely to explain this by reference to our concern and willingness to share with less fortunate others, and less likely to say that we only did it because someone shamed us into it. On the other hand, if we do something with a bad outcome, we are less likely to explain it by referring to bad properties of ourselves, and more likely to offer an explanation in terms of forces and circumstances beyond our control: for example, 'I had no choice. I had to do it because ...' and so on.

These functional biases in explanation exist; they are common everywhere; and there is an established body of research into how they operate. None the less, it is still quite common for drug workers to attempt to shed light on the nature of addiction by asking drug-users *why* they use drugs, why they continue to relapse, why they stopped using, and so forth.

Drug use and theft

In the recent study by Hammersley *et al.* (1989) we attempted to explore the relationship between drug use and crime, particularly theft. The prevailing view is that once someone starts using a drug, (for example, heroin) addiction rapidly and inevitably follows. This will be characterized by, amongst other things, intense craving to use the drug, fuelled by agonizing withdrawal symptoms if the drug is not obtained. For these reasons, the drug user's escalating habit can only be funded by illegal means, forcing the user into a life of crime almost against his or her will.

In the study just mentioned, data were collected from drug users both in and out of prison. Information on a variety of variables was collected, including drug use history, prior criminal involvement, and social and demographic information. As part of the research, we asked them to tell us why they stole; not surprisingly, they gave accounts which centred around the notion of the helpless addict, enslaved to a substance which forced them to commit their crimes. On the other hand, when we examined the other data using a statistical technique called 'regression' (a kind of mathematical sum used to find out how well something predicts something else) a different picture emerged. Theft amongst drug users was predicted best by their prior criminal experience, and hardly at all by the extent of their drug use.

In other words, the reasons given by the drug users when asked directly 'why' they stole were quite different from the factors which actually related to their criminal activities. With hindsight, of course, it is possible to see why this should be so. It is difficult to imagine any sensible reason for a drug user in prison to attribute acts of theft to anything other than the drug. And clearly, an answer such as 'I steal on purpose, just like anyone else who steals' has no function for someone in that situation.

Patterns of explanation

Coggans and Davies (1988) showed functionality in the explanations offered by drug users in a rather different kind of study. A group of heroin users were divided into two groups on the basis of their pattern of consumption. Those who used everyday (chronic users) were compared with those who used on a sporadic basis, and differences in total consumption between the groups were removed (in statistical terms, 'partialled out') by the analysis. The two groups could to some degree be differentiated on the basis of the explanations they offered for various aspects of their addiction, and these explanations were predictable. For example, the chronic group were more likely to use an explanation involving the dimensions of *internality* and *stability*, the two central features of the 'addiction' stereotype. On the other hand, the sporadic users were more likely to attribute their use to *external unstable* factors, implying luck and circumstances. The study showed, therefore, that the type of explanation offered 'made sense of' the pattern of use. After all, a chronic user can hardly explain his or her use in terms of 'bad luck' every day of the week, and a sporadic user can hardly make use of the 'helpless addict' stereotype. Accordingly, in this study, knowing the pattern of use amounted to some degree to knowing the explanation that would be offered. However, a problem remained. Were these patterns of explanation real, long-term attempts to make sense of a particular situation, which would remain stable in all circumstances? Or would they vary according to the context of the interview and subjects' knowledge of how they had been classified by the experimenter?

To answer this latter question, we carried out another study in which it was revealed to subjects how they had been classified. In this case, if answers were primarily functional, we should be able to see clear trends in the nature of the explanations offered, and furthermore predict what the nature of the explanations would be.

The study by McAllister and Davies (1991) showed how clinical classification affected the explanations given by a group of smokers. In this study, women smokers were interviewed on two occasions. At the first interview, they completed a 'diary' of their previous week's smoking and were also asked to select a preferred explanation for their smoking from a list of 'attributions', or possible reasons. At this time, there were no important differences between the explanations preferred by the light and heavy smokers in the sample. Some seven weeks later, the women were interviewed again, but this time the heavy smokers were told they had been classified as such and the words 'Heavy Smoker' appeared on each page of the schedule. Similarly, the light smokers were told of their classification, and their schedule bore the words 'Light Smoker'. Asked once more to choose an appropriate explanation, the heavy smokers now favoured attributions implying addiction, while the light smokers favoured explanations implying control. In other words, knowledge of how the therapist saw *them* had a fundamental effect on the way they preferred to explain their behaviour. It goes without saying that most people in a clinical transaction can safely assume that the therapist in turn assumes they are there because they have some fundamental problem with their drugs. Consequently, a particular mode of self-explanation is appropriate to that transaction: namely, the addiction stereotype. Other kinds of evidence exist (Brisset, 1988; Oldman, 1978) to suggest that people with particular predilections for drink, drugs, gambling or whatever change from the 'language' of volition and control to the 'language' of helplessness and addiction precisely when they encounter a serious problem which necessitates their coming into contact with outside agencies. Once again, the functional nature of explanation is revealed.

SOURCES AND IMPLICATIONS OF THE MYTHS

In the preceding paragraphs, a number of specific examples have been provided to illustrate the fact that people's verbal accounts of themselves, what they do, what they did in the past, and why, are acts of construction in a cognitive sense. Verbal reports are not so much a guide to the way the world is as an indication of how people see it and interpret it. Furthermore, their accounts are filtered and edited in the interests of self-presentation.

These facts are hardly new, and the findings are certainly not specific to drug users or other deviant groups. Every one of us edits, constructs, accentuates and minimizes every time we are asked to account for ourselves. However, in the case of drug users, where the behaviours concerned are seen generally as 'bad', there is an emphasis on forms of presentation that minimize blame and personal responsibility. Consequently, verbal accounts from drug users are more likely to place an emphasis on factors which imply helplessness, such as certain supposed pharmacological properties of drugs, insufferable life stress, family disruption, genetic predisposition and so forth, all of which explanations imply that the behaviour is due to forces which cannot be controlled. By contrast, accounts which stress drug use within a context of decision-making, choice and volition will be thin on the ground, because they imply responsibility and blame.

It seems likely that many, or possibly most, drug users take drugs primarily because they find the experience pleasurable, and because they find using drugs a sensible and rational choice, given the choices available to them. People, after all, drink for exactly these reasons and it would be strange if the dynamics of one type of drug use had nothing in common with another. When there is reliance upon drug users' verbal reports as a primary source of information about the nature of drug-using behaviour and the motives that underlie it, simultaneously with a climate of moral and legal censure surrounding drug use, then it is not surprising that the volitional and purposive aspects of drug use fail to emerge. To put it simply, there is no pay-off or advantage to drug users in adopting such a position.

Unfortunately, the general adoption of the 'helpless junkie' description has major implications for policy at all levels. Firstly, drug-using behaviour is characterized as basically different from 'normal' behaviour, and can therefore be discounted as having any social or symbolic significance. Whilst the rest of the world does things 'on purpose', drug users do things because they 'have to'. Thus they need 'treatment' rather than better choices. More importantly, though, drugs come to be seen as having magical properties, in particular the capacity to enslave and degrade, and therefore society has to be protected from the devastating properties of the substances involved *by whatever means are necessary*. From such a base, it is possible to end up with sentencing and enforcement policies which are more dangerous and disruptive to society than the drugs themselves could ever be.

SUMMARY

Chapter 3 has dealt in some detail with the beliefs that surround drugs and addiction and has described certain aspects of this belief system as mythical. These myths were explored in two ways, firstly by looking at the role of the media in helping to perpetuate stereotyped views about the power of drugs and the helplessness of addicts; secondly, by looking at the functional nature of verbal reports based on helplessness and compulsion for those who encounter problems related to their drug use.

With respect to the media, it is clear that stories about drugs that corrupt and junkies who are enslaved to their habit attract better audiences than stories of people who cope with their drug use and experience no problems. No matter what efforts are made to try and present different perspectives, the regular re-statement of the same worn-out messages ensures that the stereotype remains in general circulation and continues to be influential.

With respect to the functionality of these stereotyped beliefs, a number of research studies were cited which clearly show that drug users, and others, explain their behaviour in certain kinds of ways according to circumstances. Specifically, drug users make use of explanations that imply compulsion in situations where it makes sense for them to do so.

4

WHAT CAN TEACHERS AND PARENTS DO TO PREVENT DRUG PROBLEMS?

In previous chapters we have seen how prevalent drug use is and the extent to which the mythology does not accurately reflect reality. This chapter looks specifically at prevention strategies and the effectiveness of drug education. In the United Kingdom, as in many other countries, education is part of a multi-faceted strategy for tackling drug use. The other responses include controlling availability by reducing supplies through more effective policing and strengthening deterrents through the courts.

Before looking at specific drug-education strategies and discussing their effectiveness we should define what we mean by drug education, which varies both in the form that it takes and in its intended outcome, so that a simple definition ('to inform people about drugs') does not do justice to the variety evident in contemporary drug education.

DRUG EDUCATION: DIFFERENT APPROACHES

If there is one major banner under which all drug education operates it is *to prevent, through education, people from harming themselves by drug use*. However, under this heading differences in intended outcomes can be found, namely, education designed to prevent people coming to harm from drug use *by never starting to use drugs in the first place* (known as 'primary prevention') or education designed to prevent people from coming to harm *by using their preferred drug(s) in a safe and hygienic manner* (known as 'harm-reduction'). Clearly these are two very different sorts of drug education. We shall concentrate on primary prevention, with a brief examination of the harm-reduction approach afterwards.

Persuading people to live a 'healthy' life would seem to be quite straightforward. We have all heard or read stories of the supposedly dangerous and unpleasant side-effects of drug taking: perhaps all we need to do is to ensure that everyone knows about the more frightening side-effects and that will be sufficient to deter potential drug users from ever starting. Or, if we prefer not to be too emotive, maybe all we need to do is let the facts speak for themselves: ensure that the known facts about drug use are widely disseminated through information campaigns and people will see the sense in not taking drugs.

On the face of it, these two approaches ('fear-arousal' and 'information-based' drug education, respectively) are simply common sense. However, common sense does not take account of differences in attitudes and values that exist throughout society. In fact, 'common sense' is itself influenced by attitudes and knowledge, so that what is common sense for one person may be utter nonsense for someone else. Also, we have seen in Chapter 3 that much of what we know about the horrific side-effects of drug use is mythology. With the benefit of hindsight, based on evaluative studies of drug-education programmes utilizing the above strategies, it is now known that fear arousal is largely ineffective and that information-based campaigns can even be counterproductive. In fact these approaches have largely been superseded by what is generally known as the 'life skills' approach, which we shall discuss shortly.

FEAR-AROUSAL AND INFORMATION-BASED STRATEGIES

Fear arousal has often been used in the past in persuasive attempts to prevent people from using drugs. It is a strategy with a long history (see, for instance, some of the anti-alcohol messages of the temperance movement earlier this century). However, during the 1970s drug-education strategies changed, with the growing tendency to see fear-arousal campaigns as ineffective and alienating (Le Dain, 1970; Smart and Fejer, 1974).

In a report now famous in the field of drug education, De Haes and Schuurman (1975) tested different methods of drug education. The results showed that pupils did not stop using drugs as a result of *any* drug education, but there were other differences in effects. While none of the approaches reduced the numbers of pupils starting to use drugs, there were indications that fear-arousal and information strategies *increased* experimentation. The researchers concluded that drug-education programmes based on factual or scare tactics had a stimulating effect on drug experimentation. It seems that any drug education which emphasizes one or other drug (including education aimed at reducing alcohol consumption, see Bagnall and Plant, 1988), particularly in a fear-arousal or an information campaign, is likely to be ineffective. Why is this?

First, it seems that such messages are not necessarily perceived in the way that is intended. In connection with programmes such as the recent 'Heroin screws you up' and 'AIDS and injecting' poster campaigns, a study of young people's perceptions revealed that they did not generally see the results as something that could happen to themselves. Pupils perceived the portrayed effects of drug-taking as something that happened to 'other people' or 'junkies', and in a certain sense they saw fear-arousal posters as being exciting (Coggans *et al.*, 1990). It is as though young people tend to believe there are two sorts of people, namely, junkies and non-junkies. All the pupils in the study cited saw themselves as non-junkies (and there is every reason to agree with them). On the other hand, pupils mostly thought that fear arousal would not work with junkies but would do so with non-junkies. On this latter point there is some evidence that if fear arousal does have some effect it is with those who are least likely to take drugs in any case (Finnigan, 1988).

Second, with information-based drug education, there are problems of two different sorts: (a) what the actual (as against supposed) facts about drug use reveal; and (b) the effect that drug-related knowledge has on young people. While drug use is sometimes associated with harm, in general the facts about drug use do not support the sordid picture popularly assumed to be the case. Rather, the facts mostly reveal both pleasant and not-so-pleasant results of drug use. In other words, the facts may not be as off-putting as common sense would suggest. As noted, there is evidence that information-based drug education may stimulate interest in drugs (Schaps *et al.*, 1981; De Haes and Schuurman, 1975), possibly because they are perceived as something exciting, with the potential for enhancing a young person's standing with his or her peer group.

There is clearly a need to be careful and balanced about any information included in education programmes. Not only may interest in drugs be stimulated but we have to take into account how young people interpret the information. Just as fear-arousal material can be perceived as only relevant for other people (e.g. junkies), so material presented as 'facts' may not be believed or seen as relevant to themselves. There is also the need to balance the risk of stimulating interest with the need to inform. It is better to inform with the intention of reducing potential harm than to assume that ignorance is protection enough.

The credibility of information is very important in' any discussion about drugs with adolescents, whether as part of a drug-education programme or not. In some cases, depending on the level of drug awareness in the area, teachers and parents will not be the only sources of information about drugs; they may even know less about drugs than many young people. If parents or teachers pass off dubious attitudes or popular misconceptions as 'facts', they run the risk of destroying their own credibility in the eyes of the young people they are trying to advise. Of the various social factors (family, friends, peers, social class) that influence adolescents, peer influence has been found to have a greater impact than that of the family on alcohol and other drug use (Jessor, Collins and Jessor, 1972). It must be remembered that young people are not simply influenced in a *passive* way, contrary to their own preferences. The relationship between a young person and the peer group is more complex than that. Young people *actively* engage in different behaviours associated with preferred role models, and the development of preferences either for role models or certain types of behaviour will be the product of the many and various interactions of adolescents with their immediate and broader social environment. It is therefore a self-defeating strategy for parents and teachers to say things about drugs that (young people will 'know', rightly or wrongly) are inaccurate or even nonsensical.

Being a credible source of information entails being accurate in everything that is discussed and having a willingness to acknowledge, where appropriate, that the full facts are not known. In those instances where parents or teachers realize that they do not know the full facts, the tendency to resort to reiteration of factually dubious statements or moral exhortations must be resisted, for the simple reason that it is not sound educational practice. Presenting dubious material as 'fact' carries the very real risk of destroying the credibility of any other drug-related message, even if on some occasions it is 100 per cent accurate. Having been seen as ill-informed or prejudiced on one occasion inevitably lowers a person's apparent validity on others. And in the light of the discussion about the need for credibility of information based on adequate research, it is particularly disappointing that even some of the more enlightened drug-education packages developed over the last decade still include a few instances of opinion asserted as fact.

THE LIFE SKILLS APPROACH

Drug-education programmes in the 1980s moved towards what is known as the 'life skills' model. This approach, also being used in health education in the broader sense, includes a range of educational strategies: role-playing, developing assertiveness, and 'decision-making' skills. Life skills programmes include cognitive, affective and behavioural components that attempt (a) to equip young people with the interpersonal skills to resist direct social pressure to try or take drugs; (b) to influence positively affective or cognitive factors presumed to mediate likelihood of drug use, such as self-confidence or self-esteem, self-assertion, decision-making and communication skills. In addition, emphasis is often given to increasing awareness of alternatives. While some such programmes are based on social or personal inadequacy models of drug use, most accept that peer pressure or the desire to gain the social 'benefits' of becoming involved in local drug scenes are potent motivations towards drug use.

The rationale underlying the life skills approach stems from the perspective which sees smoking, drinking and other drug use as behaviour that is learned in a social context and is functional. Furthermore, such behaviour results from a complex interaction between characteristics of the individual and characteristics of his or her social environment (Jessor and Jessor, 1977).

Coupled with this rationale is the observation that correlations have been found between different forms of drug use such as alcohol, tobacco and marijuana use (Botvin *et al.*, 1984). It should be noted, however, that it is one thing to correlate alcohol and tobacco use with use of marijuana in a group of marijuana smokers. It is quite another thing to predict the use of 'harder' drugs such as heroin on the basis of marijuana, tobacco or alcohol use. One possible implication of such correlations is that similar predisposing factors underlie experimentation with different drugs, and that it will be more effective to employ an approach that increases awareness of alternatives, enriches self-concepts, and imparts interpersonal skills to reject drugs. This has given rise to the development of drug-education packages that seek to heighten problem-specific skills within the context of wider programmes which also address general life skills. Although a step in the right direction, in drug-education terms, two aspects of this approach are open to debate. First, when we talk of decision-making do we mean decision-implementation? And second, what is the role of self-esteem in drug use?

It is appropriate to consider what exactly is meant by the term 'decision-making' in this context, as it is ambiguous. Clearly certain aspects of the packages are more about decision-implementation than decision-making, the decision being implicit or explicit in the package content. This directive aspect could be counter-productive if perceived by the pupil as being simply moralistic and opinion-based. There is a difference between making a decision *of your own* and recognizing that the circumstances in which you find yourself *require the decision that you have been taught is appropriate in these circumstances.* The latter definition is essentially directive in that young people are taught what decision they should make. It is potentially problematic in that many young people may realize that they are not really being helped to enhance their decision-making skills as such: rather they are being told what to do. This realization will almost certainly produce some degree of resentment and thus fail to achieve the desired result.

An assumption underlying much drug education is that young people experiment with drugs because they are in some way lacking in self-esteem or are socially inadequate. While there is some evidence that people with positive health practices have higher self-esteem, high self-esteem – or even positive health practices – do not necessarily preclude use of drugs. There are two problems with the low self-esteem hypothesis. First, low self-esteem may simply be *associated* with drug use, in some individuals, with the causal connection unclear at best; second, self-esteem is usually measured with questionnaires, and such procedures are open to the same criticisms of validity and reliability as questions and answers in other psychological areas.

The more sophisticated life skills programmes integrate drugs into health education and a wider range of hazard-related behaviours. The less sophisticated life skills programmes focus only on drugs and carry the clear moral injunction to say 'no' if offered drugs. It seems intuitively obvious that telling young people that they should always reject the offer of drugs (and that that is what the new life skills are for) is less subtle than a programme which informs in a less directive manner about the consequences, good and bad, of drug use in the context of an integrated and wide-ranging positive health choice curriculum.

HARM-REDUCTION

In contrast to the primary prevention methods discussed above there is a drug educational approach that tackles the issue of how to reduce the potential for harm associated with the use of illegal drugs. This 'harm-reduction' approach has gathered some momentum with the advent of the acquired immune deficiency syndrome (AIDS) and the spread of the human immuno-deficiency virus (HIV) amongst 'at-risk' populations, which include intravenous drug users. It should be noted, however, that the harm-reduction approach is relevant to all forms of drug use whether intravenous drug use or drinking alcohol. For instance, we are familiar with education designed to cut down on alcohol-related problems, ranging from campaigns aimed at generally sensible drinking levels to campaigns which seek to persuade people not to drink and drive.

It is indicative of the seriousness with which HIV and AIDS are taken that the latter years of the 1980s saw the implementation, in a number of areas, of services for problem drug users that aim principally to lessen the risk of contracting HIV rather than primarily to stop people using drugs. Indeed, the advent of HIV and AIDS has brought about a major reassessment of policy towards drugs and drug users in the UK. Already the period 1986–89 has been identified as one of 'crisis and transformation' in British responses to drug problems with the emergence of a new 'public health paradigm of drug use' (Stimson, 1990). This new paradigm is characterized by key differences from previously prevailing services in that the main problem with drug use is seen as injection (or certain injection practices to be more precise) and that the task is to change hazardous drug-use behaviour rather than simply attempt to make existing users drug free.

Parents concerned about the possible dangers of drug use should consider whether their children's needs are better met by a policy that keeps them in contact with health professionals or by a policy that discourages them from such contact. Perhaps the starker dilemma is between having a son or daughter who uses drugs and is HIV-free on the one hand and one who contracts HIV/AIDS through intravenous drug use. For parents of young people who are definitely non-users there is always the danger of HIV being sexually transmitted should that young person have sexual intercourse with an infected person. After all, while most young people will not become intravenous drug users, most young people will form one or more sexual relationships. To change the apocryphal anti-drugs slogan, *Drugs are not death – AIDS is.*

As an approach harm-reduction has its place in the range of practical and pragmatic responses required of society. It is of necessity varied as it has to take account of different drugs and drug-use practices. In form it ranges from government-sponsored poster campaigns to highlight the link between injecting and AIDS, through individual counselling and advice, to specially designed 'comics' which use a comic format to put over safe drug use and safe sex messages. Such comics often employ what many would consider vulgar language and explicit material. Whether it is necessary to use this format, or whether it is ultimately a patronizing approach, remains to be seen. In essence the harm-reduction issue boils down to informing, in whatever way is effective, about the safe ways to use drugs. Given that no society past or present has ever found a way of preventing people from using drugs, harm-reduction is an issue that cannot be ignored, whatever our personal views are on legal or illegal drug use.

HOW EFFECTIVE IS DRUG EDUCATION?

When considering the effectiveness of drug education it is necessary to address different aspects of the question. In what way do we mean 'effective'? For instance, are we referring to ease of use for teachers, or ease of use with pupils (which can pose different questions than ease of use for teachers), or do we mean does drug education prevent young people from taking drugs?

Drug-education packages provide clear guidelines for teachers to follow in both content and delivery, which will facilitate package uptake and usage. With teachers at present being involved in many different educational initiatives, ease of use is clearly an advantage for implementation. A good package in the hands of sensitive teachers can provide the basis for a valuable adjunct to the curriculum. The corollary is, however, that there may be a failure to take account of local cultural and social circumstances. In some areas illegal drug use is considered more 'normal' than in others. If teachers are insensitive to this and are judgemental about drug users, in a negative way, then the reaction from pupils could be to discount everything offered in relation to drugs, because the teachers are seen as being 'against' their friends or even family. Of course such insensitivity could be a problem in any school, but it would be most marked in areas of higher drug use. After all there are young people in some areas who know from direct experience that heroin or cocaine does not necessarily cause personal and social disintegration.

Evaluating drug education

The purpose of carrying out an evaluation of drug education is to determine whether it works or not. However, there are two main categories of evaluation research: outcome and process evaluations (sometimes also known, respectively, as summative and formative research). Outcome evaluations ask the question 'Does it work?' while process evaluations ask 'How does it work?' Both forms of evaluation can help to refine programmes by giving feedback on aspects such as how participants react, how the trainers are carrying out their tasks, and if the actual programme resembles what was envisaged by the programme developers. In other words *process* evaluations can help to develop and refine programmes of drug education. *Outcome* evaluation of drug education, on the other hand, would attempt to evaluate the 'end product', or whether drug education makes people less likely to take drugs or to come to harm through the use of drugs. It is also important to be aware of process studies being presented as outcome studies; such as those that are based around questions of the 'do you think this will work' sort. Answers to such questions are meaningless in terms of efficacy in reducing drug use.

Different kinds of drug-education programmes have been implemented in the past, with varying degrees of success. In a major review of prevention programme evaluations, Schaps *et al.* (1981) found that their most important findings involved the effectiveness of programmes. All of the reports included in the review were published between 1968 and 1977. The reviewers categorized the 127 programmes they reviewed in terms of the various combinations of prevention strategies they identified. There were five basic categories:

(1) Information (including persuasion)
(2) Affective (including self-assertion, communication and decision-making skills)
(3) Information and affective (a combination of the two above)
(4) Counselling (either alone or with any of the above)
(5) Others

Examination of the outcome ratings of these drug prevention evaluations revealed that the majority (74) had had no effect on average ratings of drug use, intentions to use, and/or attitudes towards use. While 45 had had a positive effect on the drug-related outcome ratings, seven programmes had had a negative effect. Those that had a negative effect were information-based while those with a positive effect involved either affective or counselling components. It is doubtless significant that all ten programmes rated as being 'exemplary outcome studies' were coupled with 'fairly rigorous evaluation'. In contrast, many programmes were considered to have been weak in terms of content and methods; weaknesses that could have been eliminated if programme developers had coupled their development work with process and outcome evaluation.

A major weakness exists in the above review of drug education effectiveness. In an attempt to rate the impact of the different programmes 'drug-specific outcome ratings' were devised. These were average ratings of three different measures: (a) drug use, (b) intentions to use, and/or (c) attitudes toward use. As a basis for predicting drug use these three measures vary in strength. The weakest measure is that based on attitudes toward use, while the strongest is drug use. In addition, there are problems associated with self-reported drug use, i.e. whether the context in which answers were elicited influenced responses or whether reliability checks were built into the evaluations. To average these three measures suggests that they are in some sense measuring the same thing. This is clearly not the case.

Another review of outcome studies also identified problems with drug and/or alcohol education programmes. Kinder, Pape and Walfish (1980) reported that such programmes had mostly been ineffective in achieving the goals of decreasing substance use or preventing future abuse. They found in some instances that drug education could lead to increased usage. As most of the programmes reviewed by Kinder *et al.* were information based it can be concluded that an information-only approach tended not to reduce drug use and sometimes had effects counter to those intended.

In general, reviews of drug-education strategies that emphasized either information-giving or fear arousal have concluded that such strategies had little or no effect on drug-using behaviour (De Haes and Schuurman, 1975; Schaps *et al.* 1981). Reliance on a single educational strategy appears to be insufficient. In addition, there is the need to tailor educational programmes to take account of the factors, both cultural and social, relevant to the target population (Reid and Massey, 1986).

Results of a recent study

Recently the Scottish Education Department funded a national evaluation of drug education in Scotland (Coggans *et al.*, 1990). This major undertaking involved 106 secondary schools throughout Scotland. This initial sample was representative of Scottish secondary schools and formed a quarter of the total number of schools. It was possible to identify particular schools for the purposes of asking specific questions, such as 'Does the amount of drug education affect pupils' levels of drug-related knowledge or their likelihood of taking drugs?' In total, 1,197 pupils completed comprehensive questionnaires. It should be noted that the answers obtained with these questionnaires were found to be highly reliable.

A series of process measures suggested that pupils have some positive perceptions of drug education. However, the outcome measures showed that drug education had relatively little impact. None the less, it is worth noting that for the bulk of the pupils in the study, illegal drug use was not part of their lives. Only low levels of use were reported, with higher levels for alcohol and tobacco. It is also important to note that drug education was *not* associated with *increased* drug use on any measure.

The actual impact of drug education was assessed on a number of outcome measures, namely drug-related knowledge, perceptions and attitudes, and pupils' self-reported drug use. Other background variables were taken into consideration: age, sex and social class. The direct effect of each was assessed while controlling for the confounding effects of the other background variables. The factors that had an effect on the outcome variables examined were, in descending order of importance, age, sex, social class and drug education. Drug education had an effect on only two of the outcome variables, both of which were aspects of drug-related knowledge.

The impact of drug education on drug use appeared to have been neutral. However, levels of illegal drug use in the sample were very low. On the other hand, use of alcohol and tobacco was higher and, given that the intention of drug education in general was to have a broad impact in terms of all drugs, legal and illegal, it is of some interest that drug education did not have an effect on consumption of these (legal) drugs.

The finding that drug education had a positive influence on levels of drug-related knowledge supported the view of the vast majority of teachers that pupils knew more about drugs as a consequence of drug education. In the case of drug-related attitudes the outcome finding did not support the majority view of school staff that pupils were more anti-drugs as a result of drug education. On average, the young people in the study had fairly stereotypical drug-related perceptions and attitudes. Where reported drug-taking was concerned the findings of the study were at variance with the majority of school staff, who believed that pupils would be less likely to take drugs as a result of drug education. This study found that there was no detectable effect of drug education either to increase or decrease drinking, smoking, solvent abuse or illegal drug use.

SUMMARY

Chapter 4 has reviewed the various approaches to drug education which have been tried at different times and in different places, and has made reference to several studies which have attempted to evaluate their effectiveness. First, it is apparent that some of the received wisdom about drug education has little or no substantive basis. For example, studies have shown that in a number of ways certain types of drug education can actually make the situation worse, so that good intentions cannot in themselves be taken to guarantee beneficial outcomes. In other words, doing *something* does not necessarily have to be better than doing *nothing*. It can actually be worse if the materials are inappropriate. There is little evidence to suggest that approaches based either on fear arousal or on straightforward information-giving are likely to prove successful. On the other hand, developments of the 'life skills' approach seem more promising and clearly warrant further detailed study.

Results were cited from the National Evaluation of Drug Education in Scotland, which assessed various aspects of drug education, their implementation and their effectiveness. In general terms, there was no evidence to suggest that drug education had any impact either on pupils' attitudes towards drugs and drug users or on their self-reports of drug use. However, there was evidence suggesting that those who received drug education were slightly better informed on drug-related matters than those who received no (or less) drug education, and no evidence that the exercise had been counterproductive. In addition, the data suggested that drug-education packages themselves were only one component in a drug-education 'system', which involved characteristics of particular schools, including the degree of commitment of different teachers and relationships between staff, and between staff and pupils.

5

THE WAY FORWARD

THE BALL AND CHAIN

There is no doubt whatsoever that people can harm themselves seriously in a variety of ways by becoming involved in a cycle of excessive drug use. However, the point has also been made that harm arising from the substances themselves is not inevitable: indeed far more people use drugs than experience harm.

The way forward consists of learning to contemplate alternative accounts of drug misuse that do not rely on the central tenet of 'addiction'. In its place, we require a conception based on dynamic and purposive choices, which are volitional if not always wise. This contrasts with a view that in principle denies the ability to choose, in the context of a process whose outcome is determined by the pharmacology of drugs and the physiology of the user: a closed system. The difference is primarily philosophical, and the contention of this book is that empirical evidence exists supporting the need for a switch to a new philosophy. The new philosophy is more challenging, as it removes the basic crutch on which the 'addiction' notion rests and describes it as a functional form of explanation which is social in origin. The problem is that such a conception is unwelcome to those whose personal drug or alcohol problems have been solved in terms of the old philosophy; it is easy to see why a new approach stressing personal responsibility should appear highly threatening. The 'twelve-step' ideology still resides at the heart of many treatment approaches, the best known of these being Alcoholics Anonymous. Within this approach the addict is seen as suffering from a disease. Much controversy has raged over the disease notion, perhaps the most notable contributions coming from Heather and Robertson (1981; 1985). It is significant that within this species of therapy the addict never recovers but is always 'recovering'.

Certainly, the twelve-step or AA type of approach works for many people, though Heather and Robertson have pointed out that there are also many people who cannot accept the basic premises and for whom it therefore has nothing to offer. However, to concede that the approach 'works' implies principally that drinking ceases. In other respects, the approach is less successful. In particular, the fact that abstinence is predicated on a conviction instilled by the treatment regime, that the sufferer has a disease over which he or she has no control, necessitates abstinence as the only goal feasible. In other words, abstinence is supported by a conviction on the part of the sufferer that he or she is still an addict and will always be one, liable at any time to fall under the spell of particular substances and their pharmacology. The person is not therefore 'cured' of an addiction, but rather the reverse. He or she is actually *confirmed* as an addict; that belief is the lynch-pin for a lifetime of abstinence. Remove the lynch-pin, and the edifice starts to crumble. Small wonder that people become anxious and angry when the sand upon which their castle of abstinence is erected is given a few pokes. Clearly, a more durable and resilient route to coping with drug problems is required.

The twelve-step model, involving denial of personal responsibility and the need to draw strength from some higher power, thus leads to a cessation of drug use sustained by a central belief system which some individuals can accept, but others cannot. If one has problems with 'higher powers', one requires advice about alternative sources of strength. However, even for those who can accept the necessary belief system, the price to pay is the ball and chain referred to at the head of this section. Namely, a lifetime of abstinence predicated on the belief that there is an area of one's existence where one's behaviour is machine- or automaton-like; that a range of substances exists to which one will inevitably react like a leaf before a storm rather than a human being confronted by choices. The person is not therefore liberated from a cycle of harmful use, but merely relocated within the 'addiction system'. Instead of being a 'junkie' who uses drugs, he becomes a 'junkie' who, one day at a time, does not use drugs. But still a 'junkie', still helpless in the face of forces that are impossible to overcome.

WHAT ABOUT THE PHARMACOLOGY OF DRUG ACTION?

It is important to understand that adoption of a new approach does not mean that the pharmacology of drug action is either neglected or ignored. Drugs clearly have effects at many levels; indeed their impact on the central nervous system, and their capacity to modify neural transmission and other processes, gives them the particular pleasurable effects which are deliberately sought by the user. The fact that they have these effects explains why people want to use them, though the role of enjoyment in motivating drug use of all kinds is frequently overlooked in the search for a different kind of explanation. It is sufficient to note that major texts (e.g. Bowman and Rand, 1980; Balfour, 1990) exist on the pharmacology of drug action, and an entire area of research investigates exactly what pharmacological impact different drugs have.

However, the pharmacology of drug-taking is not the same as the pharmacology of decision-making, and does not replace it. The evidence that drugs have very real effects is not evidence that drug users do things because they *have to* in circumstances where the rest of the world *does not have to*. Perhaps the last word should come from a pharmacologist, since such a person is most competent to speak on this issue. In the aftermath of a conference on drugs held at the University of Strathclyde in 1990 Dr Maureen Benwell wrote the following in a letter to the organizers:

> There is just one comment I would like to make, ... and
> that is that the neural substrate thought to underlie the
> reward-related properties of drugs of abuse, namely the
> mesolimbic dopamine system, is also believed to
> subserve the appetitive phases of many goal directed
> behaviours such as eating, drinking and sex. Therefore I
> do not believe that addiction, *per se*, should be seen as a
> substance based phenomenon.

It is interesting that in the book *Excessive Appetites* Orford (1984) similarly concludes that the essential features of addicted behaviour do not reside in particular substances, on the basis of a quite different kind of evidence. What he prefers to describe as 'excessive appetites' include eating, drinking, sexual behaviour and also gambling, in addition to taking drugs. In other words, two eminent researchers, one a pharmacologist and the other a psychologist, have by quite different routes concluded that so-called 'addicted' behaviour occurs over a broad spectrum of activities that includes, but is not specific to, the ingestion of psychoactive substances. The idea that the word 'addiction' delineates a type of response to a set of pharmacological agents is thus under challenge from a number of directions, and Orford and

Benwell are by no means alone in their speculations. The challenge has the most profound implications, firstly for the ways we think about drug users and their needs, and secondly for the control policies we adopt towards drugs. It represents a 'paradigm shift', a new way of conceptualizing a problem.

A CHANGE OF HEART

So many social research endeavours seem to finish with a plea for a change of attitude that it seems somewhat trite and ineffectual to suggest a similar need here. Furthermore, since attitude change is in itself not the key to behavioural change, the plea is often misdirected in those areas where a change in behaviour is the central goal. What is required with respect to drug problems is something more fundamental than a shift in the verbal statements people make when asked some 'attitudes to drugs' questions by a survey researcher. We require a shift both in beliefs and in behaviour which is best encapsulated by the phrase 'a change of heart'. This change of heart requires that we stop reacting to drug problems with a set of beliefs and behaviours that are more appropriate to issues of life and death; as we have seen in the earlier chapters, whatever else drug use may be, it certainly does not come close to the top of any reasonable list of current life-and-death issues. The reader is reminded that illicit drug-related deaths in the UK number about 400 per annum (*Drug Scenes*, 1987) at the present time. Compared with deaths attributable to smoking, alcohol, road-traffic accidents, heart disease, accidents at work and in the home, and countless other sources of fatal injury, deaths due to illicit drugs come well down the list.

In addition, we should take close heed of the fact that whilst the drug war is being waged on the other side of the Atlantic, and we are currently showing all the signs of wanting to join in, nothing comparable takes place in Holland. According to personal communication with a leading Dutch researcher, the type of media hyperbole reserved for drug issues in the UK simply has no counterpart in Holland, and would be perceived as ridiculous. At the same time, the same research worker has data on cocaine use in Amsterdam (Cohen, 1989) which shows a far less alarming, and in human terms less costly, picture than that regularly received from the USA, where there are reputed to be 40 shootings per week in Washington alone, as a consequence of the illicit cocaine trade made so lucrative by the policies being implemented there. Furthermore, even in the United States there are voices raised in protest about the drug 'war'. A telling quote from Professor Ernest Drucker, head of a drug treatment programme in New York, reads: 'No wonder drug and AIDS experts come to New York from all over the world to see how not to handle this epidemic' (Drucker, 1990).

At all levels, therefore, we have to overhaul our beliefs and behaviours towards drug problems. Otherwise, our over-response can create side-effects more damaging to society than the drugs themselves. Illicit drugs can be dangerous, but they do not have to produce death and disaster on the streets if we adopt rational and balanced strategies towards their use at an individual level and government policies that permit such strategies to be implemented.

This, however, raises a fundamental question for concerned parents, whether they be parents with a drug-using child or simply parents worried by that possibility. Where a youngster has been caught dabbling in drugs, the pressures operate in such a way as to push those involved into adopting the 'addiction' stereotype in return for some sort of societal and medical 'absolution'. It is far easier to say 'Amanda takes drugs because she is sick and can't help it,' than 'Amanda takes drugs on purpose because she likes it', especially if Amanda is standing in front of the magistrate at the time. It is easy to see that, in such circumstances, the difficulties of preserving an objective and dispassionate view cannot be overemphasized.

Such absolution, however, is quite unnecessary, and far from being helpful it makes the situation worse. It persuades all concerned that they are battling with powers beyond their capacity to control, attaches very sticky labels, and sets prescriptions for courses of action that will embed Amanda further in the drug-addiction system rather than disembedding her from it. However, the advantages of adopting the inaccurate stereotypes are manifest, so how is one to react when the drug problem comes home to roost?

PRACTICAL CONSIDERATIONS

In most situations there are a number of choices available. For example, whilst services are available for those with drug problems on a national level which offer counselling and advice and occasionally other services, they are not all the same. Despite training courses for drug counsellors, there is variability in the advice they provide.

We verified this on a small scale by asking one of our researchers to phone different agencies and report that he had been using the drug 'ecstasy' on and off for some weeks and was worried about the possible consequences. The results were interesting. Firstly, some agencies were unclear about what it was and failed to make any connection between ecstasy and MDMA (methyldioxymethampheta- mine). More important, however, was the advice given. It was de- scribed on the one hand as being highly addictive and having danger- ous side-effects, and the advice was that use should cease immediately to avoid disastrous consequences. The danger of with- drawal was stressed, and it was asserted that all drugs produced basically the same kind of awful withdrawal symptoms. On the other hand, another agency advised that there would probably be no ser- ious consequences given the level of use reported, that it was unlikely that the researcher would become addicted, but that some elementary precautions and controls made sense if he was determined to carry on using it.

In another of our studies, we discovered a school where pupils with drug and other problems were counselled by teachers, and given advice on how to deal with family difficulties. The parents were actively involved, and pupils with problems were sometimes actually tracked down by teaching staff in the local housing scheme, in an effort to keep them attending school and leading as normal a life as possible. In contrast, we found another school where any pupil found using drugs was referred to a local psychiatric hospital for 'treatment'. As a parent, one ought to react with some dismay to the suggestion that any child who uses drugs is automatically 'sick' and needs psychi- atric help; yet, apparently, some people were actually reassured by this procedure.

A salutary lesson comes from a study in Glasgow by two psychia- trists, Sourindhrin and Baird (1984). In this study, a clinic was estab- lished at a police station in the East End of Glasgow, in response to frightening reports about the dangers of glue and solvent sniffing and tales of physical dependence amongst 10- to 15-year-olds. Between October 1978 and December 1980, all children found to be involved in solvent abuse within the area of jurisdiction were automatically referred to the clinic. The report deals with 300 children below 16 years of age, who attended the clinic during the study period. The authors write, 'The facets of the study which are of central interest are: the role of the police; the apparent resolution of the activity; *the lack of physical damage; the very low incidence of associated psychiatric disorder*, and the association with paternal unemployment and single parent families' (emphasis added).

The important point from the study is that the group in question forms a more representative cross-section than do normal clinic populations, by virtue of the very broad manner of referral. What is revealed is that most of the children referred had suffered no physical damage and did not require psychiatric treatment. It was also revealed that many of them came from disrupted or economically deprived families.

If we find ourselves, as parents, in the position of having a drug user for a son or daughter, we should think carefully before accepting, or opting for, an 'illness' or 'sick' conceptualization. It might make us feel easier in our minds, it provides a comforting mode of explanation, and it makes us more likely to receive sympathy from our friends if we tell them about it. But the longer-term price to be paid by the son or daughter may be terrible; people never escape from the 'addiction' label, once it has been pinned on hard enough.

When faced with this distressing situation, therefore, the answer is to shop around and find out what is available; not to opt for the first lifeline that is thrown, because some of these may pull in the wrong direction. Few teenagers are heavily into drugs, and the prognosis for those who are is generally better than for older age-groups with a longer history of drug use. The key word in all this is probably 'normal', and parents should search for the type of help that makes minimal use of medical concepts and terminology, rejecting any suggestion that the young drug user is *de facto* sick, addicted, or helpless. It seems wise to accept help only from those with a more dynamic view of drug use, who can use concepts of control and decision-making, and who reject the stereotype, wherever it is possible to do so.

A CHANGE OF EDUCATIONAL PRACTICE

Over the past decade, a lucky-bag of approaches to drug education for children has been adopted. We have already noted in Chapter 4 that some outcome studies have revealed negative effects of certain types of drug education, and since many endeavours are not capable of evaluation it is difficult to gauge the damage that may have been caused by some kinds of inappropriate drug education. One wonders about the advisability, for example, of education hinging on demonstrations of drug use, injecting techniques and so forth, aimed at classes of ordinary schoolchildren, which were favoured in a number of places at times in the past.

On the other hand, many of us wrongly believe that education which centres on the attempt to scare youngsters out of any interest in drugs is a good way to go about it; this remains a clear public conviction (Finnigan, 1988) in spite of the evidence that such an approach has a constrained applicability. Despite a developing strand of educational theory stressing choice, self-determination and life skills, drug education at the level of the national campaign still makes regular use of inaccurate and stereotypical perceptions of drug use and ill-advised moral stances. In general terms those educational initiatives which look most promising are non-prescriptive, non-scaremongering, non-moralizing, factually accurate, and are not drug-specific. This contrasts with the content of national campaigns which still remain drug focused, moral, frightening, highly prescriptive, and sometimes factually misleading.

However, our researches suggest that the *content* of drug education, whilst important, is not the only crucial factor in the system. Our own data from the National Evaluation of Drug Education in Scotland indirectly suggest that some schools achieve things in this troubled area that other schools do not. The word 'system' is used deliberately above, as an antidote to current drug education which has become more and more 'package based'. It is now impossible to keep up to date with the plethora of packages available, all recommended by somebody and all able to produce data to suggest that they work, even where such data frequently do not stand close scrutiny. The search resembles the search for the Holy Grail. The belief appears to be that someone, somewhere, will finally produce the package that does the trick, and all we need to do is keep producing more and more packages until we find it.

In fact, it must be obvious to anyone that the success of any such educational endeavour depends not simply on package content, but on the rest of the 'system'. The analogy that springs to mind comes from gardening. No matter how refined and productive *in principle* the strain of seed to be sown, nothing will come of it without a productive growing medium. In the current example, the growing medium is the school itself; how it works; how teachers relate to other staff and to pupils; how much serious and careful effort is put in; the extent to which health and social education is seen as either a timely addition to, or an unwelcome distraction from, more academic subjects, and so on. At the present time, most energy appears to be concentrated on package content and ease of use, but without attention to the school system as a whole, success if any will be haphazard and piecemeal. Unfortunately, questions about what distinguishes successful schools from unsuccessful schools and how that success manifests itself remain questions which are largely unaddressed with respect to drug education. The next step is to carry out fine-grained studies to discover what aspects of school systems provide the best basis for health and social education, including education about drugs.

A CHANGE OF POLICY

Although there is plenty of scope for new educational initiatives, especially along the lines of a whole-school or systems approach, we cannot realistically expect this to be sufficient. In the absence of impetus from new and changed policies, education alone can never suffice for the job in hand. The problem naturally arises as to how best to shape education and policy so that they complement and enhance, rather than contradict, each other. At the present time, for example, there is a clear mismatch between informed educational opinion and the views of government on how best to tackle the drug problem. Whilst a non-prescriptive and broadly based approach is preferred by the one, the other pursues a philosophically opposite line of thinking based on fear arousal and the over-estimation of the threat of death. Since drug-wise teenagers and their friends will know at first hand that drugs lead to death with rather less frequency than does riding a bicycle, the credibility of the campaign is fundamentally undermined at the start: they will know they are being conned. To the extent that this is true, other better-conceived campaigns may well be treated with suspicion.

Furthermore, once the message is accepted that drug use is not necessarily linked to decline and death, but is something that can be coped with in terms of human resources and capacities which we all possess, so other aspects of policy come under a different type of scrutiny. If the context of drug use, rather than the drugs themselves, constitutes the main danger, what function is served by the increased criminalization of drug use, when this makes the context even more extreme? The available evidence (Haw, 1989) shows that, in Scotland, the number and severity of prison sentences handed out for drug offences, particularly those involving 'possession with intent to supply', has increased dramatically over the past decade. From the position advocated in this book, such a development can only be seen as counterproductive. It brings drug users further into contact with crime and criminal expertise, which is the best predictor of drug-related theft (Hammersley *et al.*, 1989), and enmeshes drug use with general criminality even further. There is also evidence that imprisonment may lead to an increase in needle-sharing practice (Rahman, Ditton and Forsyth, 1989; McKeganey, Barnard and Watson, 1989). The availability of injecting equipment is low in prisons and therefore drug users are more likely to share needles, a practice that they maintain on release.

The question 'What happens to an incarcerated drug user, after he or she leaves prison?' is a good one to which there is no satisfactory answer at present. It is speculative that for some drug offenders, a minor drug career is transformed into a more serious drug career, accompanied by other crime, as a result of the initial gaol sentence. In the meantime, the question remains as to whether more frequent and more severe prison sentences are the best way to tackle the drug problem. The basic philosophy behind such measures appears to be that drugs constitute a fundamental threat to the life of individuals, and to society as a whole. Consequently, the drug menace has to be stamped out by whatever means prove necessary. If, however, the threat to individuals and to society posed by drugs is substantially overestimated, then the appropriateness of extreme reactions comes into doubt.

Apart from the arguments already put forward, which hinge upon the fact that the dangers of drug misuse are generally misperceived, there are purely practical considerations. The assumption behind the war on drugs is that it can succeed. That is, the war can be won and illicit drug use can be eradicated from our midst. However, both history and common sense suggest otherwise; and few things are so distressing as the sight of governments continuing to pursue a goal that cannot be attained with the mindless optimism of Tantalus trying to get a drink.

The comparison between the 'drug war' and the Prohibitionist movement in the USA is compelling; despite the fact that the analogy is imperfect in a number of ways, one need only take the point that the attempt to eradicate recreational alcohol use failed, and that death on the streets was then, as now, a major side-effect of the legislation. To argue that the two phenomena were so different that there are no points of comparison smacks of deliberate obfuscation; to argue that Prohibition was successful on the grounds that 'it did reduce the level of consumption and related problems' (Drummond, 1990) requires a high degree of selective attention that ignores the other manifest costs involved. Furthermore, the death penalty, the ultimate sanction available (one which it is hoped there will be no recourse to here, despite popular appeals in some tabloid papers to 'hang the pushers'), is already operational in some parts of the world. It is not a universally successful strategy: drug use and drug trading are endemic in some countries which operate the death penalty for certain drug offences. And even where some success may be claimed, there is a dreadful irony about legislation which is more lethal than the behaviour it sets out to control.

If drugs will not go away, and all the evidence suggests that with the passage of time drug use will become more rather than less widespread, then there is little alternative to finding ways of living with them and of coping with their effects. The issue has become more acute in the last five years with the realization that intravenous drug use is associated with the advent of the HIV virus through the use of shared and contaminated needles. Anything which drives drug use further underground, and makes it less available to open and prompt intervention, promises to assist in the spread of a far more serious threat, the full extent of which is still to be realized. On this issue at least, the government has its priorities in order, with the unambiguous assertion from the Advisory Body on the Misuse of Drugs that spread of HIV is a more pressing problem than drug misuse.

If we accept the logic of the above arguments, and are in agreement that a *harm-reduction* policy directed towards people and their needs is preferable to a 'war on drugs', then it is worthwhile considering the type of policy options. Fortunately, there are a few examples of harm-reduction and other pragmatic approaches to the problems of drug misuse both at home and abroad, which merit closer scrutiny and from which lessons may be learned. For example, the approach adopted in Holland, which has in effect involved decriminalization of certain types of drug use, is seen as a practical and pragmatic way of reducing the health and other hazards of drug use. It would be a mistake to see this primarily as a 'liberal' policy with respect to drugs; the effect is to maintain a higher degree of contact with and control over drug users and drug problems than is achieved by more repressive means.

The type of selective 'decriminalization' referred to does not mean legalization, but represents a commitment to dealing with certain types of drug problems without having immediate recourse to prosecution, although maintaining considerable control over supply and access. It implies an agreement to stand back from using an immediate punitive response in order to give other things a chance to work first. As a consequence, whilst cannabis is still an illicit drug, its use and sale under most conditions are simply not prosecuted. Interestingly, evidence suggests that cannabis use has now reached its peak, and no increase in use is discernible (van de Wijngaart, 1988).

With respect to cocaine, a kind of dual policy exists (Cohen, 1989) whereby street dealing and street use are prosecuted, but use and distribution which are non-visible are generally not pursued, and cocaine is treated in much the same way as cannabis. In addition, a number of innovative strategies are employed for other drug users which bring them into contact with agencies rather than driving them underground. A 'methadone bus' tours certain districts, for example, stopping at pre-arranged places so that drug users can obtain their maintenance dose. All of these steps are seen as practical and sensible attempts to solve the drug problem and to avoid the effects of enmeshing drug use inextricably with criminality. Cohen points out the interesting comparison between Amsterdam and New York, and writes:

> Because in New York City a system of non-criminal and commercial cannabis distribution does not exist, one might expect lower prevalence figures there because of greater difficulty and risk involved in finding access to cannabis type drugs.
>
> In reality, prevalence figures for Amsterdam are lower again. In spite of considerable differences in law enforcement activities between both cities, prevalence of both cocaine and cannabis use is lower in Amsterdam.

The process referred to above is sometimes referred to as 'normalization' of drug use. Normalization of drug use takes account of the needs of the drug user, but also the need to reduce the harmful side-effects of punitive control policies. Furthermore, the needs of individuals and of society in general are addressed by preventing deterioration of both. In 1985 the Interministerial Steering Group on Alcohol and Drug Policy developed its *Drug Policy in Motion: Towards a Normalization of the Problem*, a policy subsequently adopted by the Dutch government. The policy is not one of acceptance or passive acquiescence, however, but a pragmatic strategy which aims to bring users of illegal drugs back into the mainstream of health and social care, where both drug and associated problems, including HIV, can be more effectively dealt with.

Nearer home, even more radical approaches have been tried, notably on Merseyside. Within an integrated 'normalization' programme, in which drug agencies, police and the health authority all collaborate in the pursuance of commonly agreed goals, there are strategies which certainly provoke thought. Needle exchanges, where users can obtain clean needles in a friendly and relaxed atmosphere and get a cup of coffee as well as advice about how to stay healthy while still using, differ fundamentally from some of the less accessible hospital-based exchanges, where drug users simply do not feel welcome. Furthermore, there is collaboration between drug agencies and pharmacists in the provision of maintenance for users on their preferred drug. The *initial* goal is thus not stopping use, but adopting safer use practices. By providing high-grade drugs of the users' choice, harm due to the injection of adulterants is avoided; the black-market drug scene has to keep its house in order as a consequence, since people will not buy poor drugs at high prices where better drugs are available on maintenance. Great claims are made for this system, and the preliminary monitoring exercises are promising (Newcombe and Parry, 1989), though a thorough long-term evaluation is necessary. None the less, whilst there are clearly problems with some aspects of the approach, many of the signs are encouraging. 'We don't need more hospital beds for drug users,' said one worker. 'What do we need beds for? Our users are all walking about the town.' Perhaps the single most fascinating suggestion from this radical programme is that drug users don't have to be sick. Given appropriate resources, it is possible to keep them in reasonable health, in charge of themselves and their habit, until such time as they choose to stop.

Given the difficulty of accurate assessment of drug users' problems, and a life style which attracts blame and moral outrage (see Chapter 3), the move towards more user-friendly services is to be commended. It has even been suggested by a senior Home Office medical officer that the 'initiatives currently underway may be the precursor to bringing drug misuse into the mainstream of health and social care' (Black, 1990).

There are great dangers in adopting any one approach lock, stock and barrel. It is not clear that either Amsterdam or Liverpool have 'got it right'. However, it is clear that New York and Washington have not got it right either. In these latter cases the problems arising from the implementation of punitive policies are easy to see, translated into a virile strain of drug-related crime and violence which is not a necessary accompaniment to drug use and misuse.

Arguments for or against legalization are often oversimplified, being presented in terms of outright and unfettered availability. Such an approach would replace one set of problems, arising out of illegality, with another set of problems arising out of unrestricted access to drugs. Given that the motivation to amend current drug-related legislation derives from a desire to reduce the harm associated with drug-taking, it is essential to assess any such recommendations on the basis of their potential to lessen public health hazards.

SUMMARY

Chapter 5 has attempted to draw some conclusions from the evidence presented and to make suggestions as to how best to contain and control drug problems in the future. Central to these suggestions is the need to adopt a new and modified conception of drugs, of drug users and of addiction itself. A number of specific points were made on the topics of drug pharmacology, drug education, and drug policy at a broad level. A shift in policy was advocated, from seeing the drug problem as primarily arising from the properties of substances to seeing it in terms of the decisions people make. In practical terms, this means giving more attention to the demand side of the equation and de-emphasizing control of supply as the major route to a resolution. Examples are available from other parts of the world to illustrate both the consequences of waging war on drugs and the consequences of more pragmatic approaches, based on the need to come to terms with the drugs that are in our midst and are unlikely to go away.

CONCLUSIONS

Whilst people can and do find themselves at the centre of a drug-use spiral from which no reasonable escape seems possible, using drugs remains a choice made by individuals from amongst a set of choices that are available. Consequently, better options that make more subjective sense to the individual lead to different choices and to different behaviour. The idea that people use drugs by force of metabolism, by force of pharmacology, or through the interaction of these two determinants, is a mechanistic view whose main virtue with respect to addiction is its convenience. But the convenience is illusory if we use it to imply that drug-using behaviour is qualitatively different from 'normal' choice behaviour, because one cannot hop between mechanistic and volitional explanations as a matter of convenience without raising a host of begged questions. One has to choose one's level of explanation and stick to it. Since people are both biological machines *and* existential beings, one can describe *all* their behaviour from either standpoint.

People do all sorts of things to excess, to the detriment of their health, their financial resources, their families, and so forth. Such acts include gambling, playing fruit machines, and excessive sexual behaviour, all of which occur on the borderlines of addiction (Orford, 1984). We must also consider how sculptors, musicians, businessmen and others pursue single goals which they find highly arousing and 'compelling' to their own and others' detriment. It is pertinent to ask whether these acts may not sometimes be equally 'addictive', even to the level of having pharmacological and physiological components in common with other addictions. After all, in the same way that drug addicts make excessive use of some substance and report, 'I'm an addict. I can't stop taking drugs,' we also have people up to and including prime ministers who, perhaps with a hint of pride, confess 'I'm a workaholic. I can't stop working.' There seems no logical basis for accepting one statement at face value whilst rejecting the other as metaphorical. They are both accounts of personal experience of equal status, and from the point of view of attribution theory, they are both highly functional statements within their respective contexts.

What is required is a common framework within which to conceptualize all those things that people do to the exclusion of their other duties and responsibilities.

The cognitive psychologist Daryl Bem (1972) has indeed suggested that the phrase 'I can't stop' is not a statement about inherent, and unknowable, capacities to stop doing things but rather the direct result of a person's self-observations that he or she reliably fails to do so. The statement is experiential; it describes the fact that, in certain situations, the person reliably chooses to do one thing rather than another, and that he or she is aware of that fact. 'I can't stop' merely does *social* justice to that situation.

However, the adoption of a framework for addiction that brings a wide range of drug- and non-drug-related behaviours into its remit requires two changes to our value system. Firstly, we have to compare 'commitment' with 'addiction', and solve the problem that 'addiction' appears to be primarily 'commitment' to things we disapprove of. And secondly, if we extend the notion of addiction to a broader range of behaviours which are not normally regarded as 'sick', it loses some of its current meaning. Whilst this may be a difficult step to take, we must bear in mind that recent pharmacological research suggests that there is indeed a common pharmacological substrate for choice behaviours of many different kinds and, as we have seen, some pharmacologists are now openly suggesting that addiction is not therefore substance based.

In contrast with the above, however, the traditional view based on helplessness and the pharmacology of compulsion still prevails. Because of that view, a policy orientated towards a 'war on drugs' still rules the day, the presumption being that drugs create the problem by virtue of their assumed properties, whereas people create the problems by the choices they make. Whilst some individuals use drugs to help them cope with difficult life events or stress, most people use drugs because they like them; in that sense, drug-using behaviour is again shown to be identical to other choice behaviours. People choose the most pleasurable of the alternatives that face them, provided they do not have important reasons for doing otherwise. The fact that using drugs is pleasurable hardly elevates the activity to a different plane of causality. Eiser (1982) has written, perhaps with a hint of irony, that the fact that people do things (in this specific instance cigarettes were the topic of discussion) because they find them pleasurable appears to have been lost sight of in the search for different types of explanation.

What we have to move away from, therefore, is the passive and mechanistic view of addiction in which the pleasures, needs, values and decision-making capacity of people are expressly denied. We have to allow personal responsibility back into the system; we cannot shelter behind the belief that the responsibility lies with the drugs, or with our own physiology.

The problem with such a shift is that a basic value is being challenged. Because of our Western view of causality and morality, we tend to think of people who do 'bad' things 'on purpose' as being 'guilty' and therefore as deserving punishment. We now require a more adult perspective that recognizes the obvious fact that adventurers and risk-takers of all types get themselves into trouble from time to time, on purpose, and still deserve our help. Furthermore, with respect to drugs, it is a lot cheaper and less dangerous to offer rescue to problem drug users than to air-lift mountaineers from the North Face of the Eiger or bring back a single explorer who finds himself through his own actions at the North Pole *in extremis*. Furthermore, when we bring risk-takers back from the Eiger or the North Pole, we use medical services to treat their broken limbs, their frost-bite, or whatever, but we do not judge that they require medical intervention for having decided to go to those places in the first place, though we are entitled to feel that they were perhaps unwise. Finally, we would probably take steps to reduce future risks by teaching people who wish to go out in the hills, or to climb mountains, how to minimize the risks of harming themselves.

In a roughly analogous way, new approaches to drug use concentrate on harm-reduction in a very literal sense. If we cannot persuade our drug users to stop immediately, we can at least keep them as healthy as possible until such time as they decide to do so. Least of all can we assume that by choosing to use drugs they have thereby demonstrated that something is wrong with their capacity to make decisions, though we may not like the decisions they make.

The alternative strategy of severe penalties for drug offences has two main drawbacks. Firstly, it makes drugs and drug users less amenable to control and helpful intervention, by driving the problem underground; secondly, it cannot succeed. What it does achieve is to encourage more people to enter the field of drug-related crime as the drugs themselves escalate in value at the street level, and it places a premium on drug 'territory', so that the 'war on drugs' becomes war in a broader sense.

With the close association between HIV/AIDS and intravenous drug misuse, the time is now clearly ripe for the adoption of a new conception of drug problems, and a new set of responses. We have to step back sharply from the anti-drug crusade and from the model presented by enforcement agencies in the USA, and look elsewhere for helpful advice. Part and parcel of adopting new strategies is the positive and encouraging belief that drug use is not the end of the world, that it can be controlled and that the very real dangers can be minimized by adopting certain strategies of use. For example, many of the more serious consequences of cocaine and heroin use can be substantially reduced if inducements are provided for users to smoke, or snort, drugs in preference to injection, until such time as they wish to stop altogether: a common-sense strategy which also hits straight at the HIV problem amongst drug users.

Because within the societal context illicit drug use is seen as bad, and drugs as inherently evil, there is a premium on modes of self-explanation that dissipate blame and culpability. Users and non-users become enmeshed in an unhelpful set of functional, but not real, attributions centring on helplessness and illness. Unhappily, this process gives rise to a second-order reality of our own invention. Once we have invented these functional forms of explanation, it becomes necessary to live up to them, so the mythology of addiction becomes a self-fulfilling prophecy. In other words, we can actually produce the type of drug problem we most fear.

REFERENCES

Asterisked (*) references are recommended for reading in the original.

Advisory Council on the Misuse of Drugs (1984) *Prevention*. London: HMSO.

Aitken, P. P. (1978) *Ten-to-Fourteen-Year-Olds and Alcohol*. Edinburgh: HMSO.

Anderson, I., Aitken, P. P. and Davies, J. B. (1981) Recall of the ordering of the symptoms of alcoholism. *British Journal of Clinical Psychology*, **20**, 137–8.

Bachman, J., Johnston, L. and O'Malley, P. (1981) Smoking, drinking and drug use among American high school students: correlates and trends. *American Journal of Public Health*, **71**, 59–69.

Bagnall, G. and Plant, M. A. (1988) Alcohol education: the rocky road ahead. *Alcohol and Alcoholism*, **23** (3) 191–2.

Balfour, D. J. K. (1990) *Psychotropic Drugs of Abuse*. New York: Pergamon.

Ball, J. C. (1967) The reliability and validity of interview data obtained from 59 narcotic drug addicts. *American Journal of Sociology*, **72**, 650–59.

Belson, W., Millerson, G. L. and Didcott, P. J. (*circa* 1968) *The Development of a Procedure for Eliciting Information from Boys about the Nature and Extent of Their Stealing*. London School of Economics: Survey Research Centre.

Bem, D. J. (1972) Self-perception theory. *In* Berkowitz, L. (ed.), *Advances in Experimental Social Psychology*. Hillsdale, NJ: Erlbaum.

Benwell, M. (1990) Personal communication.

Black, D. (1990) AIDS and HIV. The way forward? *British Journal of Addiction*, **85**, 350–51.

Botvin, G. J., Baker, E., Renick, N. L., Filazzola, A. D. and Botvin,

E. M. (1984) A cognitive-behavioural approach to substance abuse prevention. *Addictive Behaviours*, **9**, 137–47.

Bowman, W. C. and Rand, M. J. (1980) *Textbook of Pharmacology*. Cambridge: Blackwell.

Brisset, D. (1988) Denial in alcoholism: a sociological interpretation. *Journal of Drug Issues*, **18** (3) 385–402.

Browne, D. (1988) Crack. *Observer*, 24 July, p. 15.

Carvel, J. (Home Affairs Editor) (1990) Mellor warns of lull before drugs storm. *Guardian*, 20 March.

Chick, J. and Duffy, J. (1979) Application to the alcohol dependence syndrome of a method of determining the sequential development of symptoms. *Psychological Medicine*, **9**, 313–19.

Coggans, N. and Davies, J. B. (1988) Explanations for heroin use. *Journal of Drug Issues*, **18** (3), 457–65.

*****Coggans, N., Shewan, D., Henderson, M., Davies, J. D. and O'Hagan, F. J.** (1990) *National Evaluation of Drug Education in Scotland: Final Report*. Edinburgh: Scottish Education Department.

*****Cohen, P.** (1989) *Cocaine Use in Amsterdam*. Amsterdam: Universiteit van Amsterdam.

Davies, J. B. and Baker, R. (1987) The impact of self-presentation and interviewer bias effects on self-reported heroin use. *British Journal of Addiction*, **82**, 907–12.

Davies, J. B. and Stacey, B. (1972) *Teenagers and Alcohol*. London: HMSO.

De Haes, W. and Schuurman, J. (1975) Results of an evaluation study on three drug education models. *International Journal of Health Education*, **18**, Supplement.

Drucker, E. (1990) Through the eye of the needle, II. *International Journal on Drug Policy*, **1** (6) 10–11.

Drummond, C. (1990) Legalising drugs: whose side are you on? *'19' Magazine*, July, p. 38.

Eiser, J. R. (1982) Addiction as attribution: cognitive processes in giving up smoking. *In* Eiser, J. R. (ed.), *Social Psychology and Behavioural Medicine*. Chichester: Wiley.

Finnigan, F. (1988) *Stereotyping in Addiction: an application of the Fishbein-Ajzen theory to heroin using behaviour.* Ph.D. thesis. Glasgow: University of Strathclyde.

*__Hammersley, R., Morrison, V., Davies, J. B. and Forsyth A.__ (1989) *Heroin Use and Crime: A Comparison of Heroin Users and Non-users in and out of Prison.* Report to the Criminological Division: Scottish Home and Health Department.

Haw, S. (1989) *The Sentencing of Drug Offenders in Scottish Courts.* Report to the Criminology and Law Research Group: Scottish Home and Health Department.

Heather, N. and Robertson, I. (1981) *Controlled Drinking.* London: Methuen.

*__Heather, N. and Robertson, I.__ (1985) *Problem Drinking: The New Approach.* Harmondsworth: Penguin.

__Home Office Statistical Bulletin 24/90__ (1990) Statistics of the misuse of drugs: seizures and offenders dealt with, United Kingdom 1989. (This bulletin is updated annually.) London: HMSO.

__Home Office Statistical Bulletin 7/90__ (1990) Statistics of drug addicts notified to the Home Office, United Kingdom in 1989. (This bulletin is updated annually.) London: HMSO.

Jenkins, C. D., Hurst, M. W. and Rose, R. M. (1979) Life-changes: do people really remember? *Archives of General Psychiatry,* **36,** 379–84.

Jessor, R., Collins, M. I. and Jessor, S. L. (1972) On becoming a drinker: social-psychological aspects of an adolescent transition. *In* Seixas, F.A. (ed.), *Nature and Nurture in Alcoholism.* New York: Annals of the New York Academy of Sciences.

Jessor, R. and Jessor, S. (1977) *Problem Behaviour and Psychosocial Development: A Longitudinal Study of Youth.* London: Academic Press.

Kandel, D. (1980) Drug and drinking behaviour among youth. *Annual Review of Sociology,* **6,** 235–85.

Kinder, B. N., Pape, N. E. and Walfish, S. (1980) Drug and alcohol education programs: a review of outcome studies. *International Journal of the Addictions,* **15,** 1035–54.

References

Le Dain, G. (1970) *Interim Report of the Commission of Inquiry into the Non-medical Use of Drugs*. Ottawa: Information Canada.

McAllister, P. and Davies, J. B. (1991) Attributional shifts in smokers as a consequence of clinical classification. *Journal of Drug Issues* (under review).

McKeganey, N., Barnard, M. and Watson, H. (1989) HIV-related risk behaviour among a non-clinic sample of injecting drug users. *Journal of Addiction*, **84**, 1481–90.

McGinty, S. and Hamilton, D. (1990) Cult. Facing the facts. *Glasgow Evening Times*, 17 July, p. 5.

Newcombe, R. and Parry, A. (1989) Preventing the spread of HIV infection among and from injecting drug users in the UK: an overview with specific reference to the Mersey regional strategy. Liverpool: Mersey Regional Health Authority.

O'Doherty, F. (1988) *The Effect of Naturally Occurring Life-events on Changes in Consumption of Alcohol, Tobacco and Heroin*. Ph.D. thesis. Glasgow: University of Strathclyde.

O'Doherty, F. and Davies, J. B. (1987) Life events and addiction; a critical review. *British Journal of Addiction*, **82**, 127–37.

O'Doherty, F. and Davies, J. B. (1988) Life events, stress and addiction. *In* Fisher, S. and Reason, J. (eds), *Handbook of Life Stress, Cognition and Health*. Chichester: Wiley.

Oldman, D. (1978) Compulsive gamblers. *Sociological Review*, **26**, 349–371.

*****Orford, J.** (1984) *Excessive Appetites*. London: Wiley.

Plant, M. A., Peck, D. F. and Stuart, R. (1982) Self-reported drinking habits and alcohol related consequences among a cohort of Scottish teenagers. *British Journal of Addiction*, **77**, 75–90.

Plant, M. A., Peck, D. and Samuel, E. (1985) *Alcohol, Drugs and School Leavers*. London: Tavistock.

Rahman, M. Z., Ditton, J. and Forsyth, A. J. M. (1989) Variation in needle sharing practices among intravenous drug users in Possil (Glasgow). *British Journal of Addiction*, **85**, 923–7.

Reid, D. and Massey, D. (1986) Can school drug education be more effective? *Health Education Journal*, **45**, 7–13.

*Royal College of Psychiatrists (1987) *Drug Scenes: A Report on Drugs and Drug Dependence by the Royal College of Psychiatrists*. London: Gaskell.

Schaps, E., Di Bartolo, R., Moskowitz, J. M., Palley, C. and Chugrin, S. (1981) A review of 127 drug abuse prevention program evaluations. *Journal of Drug Issues*, **11**, 17–44.

Sheppard, M. (1984) Drug abuse prevention education: what is realistic for schools? *Journal of Drug Education*, **14**, 232–329.

Smart, R. G. and Fejer, D. (1974) The effects of high and low fear arousal messages about drugs. *Journal of Drug Education*, **4**, 225–35.

Sourindhrin, I. and Baird, J. A. (1984) Management of solvent abuse: a Glasgow community approach. *British Journal of Addiction*, **79**, 227–32.

Stimson, G. V. (1990) AIDS and HIV: the challenge for British drug services. *British Journal of Addiction*, **85**, 329–39.

Stimson, G. V. and Oppenheimer, E. (1982) *Heroin Addiction*. London: Tavistock.

Stott, D. H. (1958) Some psychosomatic aspects of causality in reproduction. *Journal of Psychosomatic Research*, **3**, 42–5.

Swadi, H. (1988) Drug and substance use among 3,333 London adolescents. *British Journal of Addiction*, **83**, 935–42.

Trebach, A. S. (1987) *The Great Drug War*. New York: Macmillan.

Woodiwiss, M. (1988) *Crime, Crusades and Corruption: Prohibitions in the United States*. London: Pinter.

van de Wijngaart, G. F. (1988) A social history of drug use in the Netherlands: policy outcomes and implications. *Journal of Drug Issues*, **18** (3) 481–95.

INDEX